Unquiet Diplomacy

UNQUIET
DIPLOMACY

Paul Cellucci

KEY PORTER BOOKS

Library and Archives Canada Cataloguing in Publication

Cellucci, Paul, 1948–
    Unquiet diplomacy / Paul Cellucci.

Includes index.
ISBN 1-55263-706-9

1. Cellucci, Paul, 1948–. 2. Ambassadors—Canada—Biography. 3. Ambassadors—United States—Biography. 4. Canada—Foreign relations—United States. 5. United States—Foreign relations—Canada. I. Title.

FC249.C42 2005   327.2'092   C2005-902730-4

THE CANADA COUNCIL | LE CONSEIL DES ARTS
FOR THE ARTS | DU CANADA
SINCE 1957 | DEPUIS 1957

ONTARIO ARTS COUNCIL
CONSEIL DES ARTS DE L'ONTARIO

The publisher gratefully acknowledges the support of the Canada Council for the Arts and the Ontario Arts Council for its publishing program. We acknowledge the support of the Government of Ontario through the Ontario Media Development Corporation's Ontario Book Initiative.

We acknowledge the financial support of the Government of Canada through the Book Publishing Industry Development Program (BPIDP) for our publishing activities.

Key Porter Books Limited
Six Adelaide Street East, Tenth Floor
Toronto, Ontario
Canada M5C 1H6

www.keyporter.com

Design: Peter Maher
Electronic formatting: Jean Lightfoot Peters

Printed and bound in Canada

05 06 07 08 09 6 5 4 3 2 1

Contents

Acknowledgments

It is a pleasure to have the opportunity to acknowledge the invaluable contributions of those whose work, advice, friendship and support made my years as ambassador to Canada both enjoyable and a time of continued positive relations despite significant challenges.

My first and deepest thanks go always to my wife, Jan, who provides support, guidance, irreverence and love. She was my best friend on this Canadian journey.

Jan and I met hundreds, in fact thousands, of wonderful people during our four years in Canada. A few of them became good friends and provided heartfelt support and advice. Jan and I are grateful for their hospitality and for introducing us to their magnificent country. Among them were former Prime Minister Jean Chrétien and Aline Chrétien and former Prime Minister Brian Mulroney and his wife Mila. Prime Minister Paul Martin and Sheila Martin, Adrian Burns and Greg Kane, and Ken and Christina Loeb all shared with us their warm hospitality and their genuine love for a country that we came to think of as home. Archbishop Marcel Gervais provided comfort and guidance when our spirits were lowest after 9/11, and shared our joy when he married our daughter Anne in Ottawa. Jan and I are blessed to call them our friends.

The embassy staff and those at the American consulates from Vancouver to Halifax were exceptional. Americans should be truly proud of the competence and character of these men and women who represent their country and its interests abroad. Steve Kelly was the deputy chief of mission for most of my time as ambassador, before he left to assume the same job in Mexico City. Steve's solid grasp of every aspect of the Canada–United States relationship and his deft touch for diplomacy helped me enormously during our years working together.

Writing this memoir was a new experience for me. I had spent over thirty years in public life, giving speeches, meeting with groups, working on legislation, and campaigning. A schedule like mine didn't leave many moments for quiet reflection. But I always kept files of news clippings. These proved invaluable in writing this memoir.

Anna Porter and Jordan Fenn of Key Porter Books were enthusiastic about this project from the beginning. Their guidance and support were invaluable as I navigated the unfamiliar waters of book publishing.

Stephen Brooks helped me enormously, transferring my random thoughts from pen to paper and sifting through the boxes of news clippings and videos that I sent him. John Gray brought his keen journalist's eye to the manuscript, as well as an experienced ear for how a story should be told.

My father died in 2003. He was my inspiration for public service. I miss him deeply but I am proud to dedicate this book to him: Argeo R. Cellucci, Jr.

Paul Cellucci
Hudson, Massachusetts
September 2005

Prologue

My time as the ambassador of the United States in Canada lasted four years, more than 1,400 days that took me to the shores of three oceans, north, east and west, from the profound and bone-chilling cold of Canadian winter to the exhausting heat of summer, from days when the relationship between the United States and Canada stood as an inspiration to the world to a few days when, frankly, it was not so inspiring.

Of those more than 1,400 days, two stood apart from all others. The first saw the terrorist attacks in the United States that forever changed our world, September 11, 2001. The second came three days later, in Ottawa. With two countries grieving and in shock, we saw an emotional celebration of the values and friendship that will forever link my country, the United States, with Canada. It was one of the most moving days of my life.

The events of September 11 will make that the day generations will recall in vivid detail—where they were and what they were doing when they first saw the astonishing pictures of passenger jets crashing into the twin towers of the World Trade Center, the devastation of part of the Pentagon, and the smoldering remains of a crashed plane in a farmer's field in Pennsylvania. Thousands had died, and the world that day woke to the terrible reality of terrorism.

Improbably, I was in Calgary, another stage in the campaign of public diplomacy on which I had embarked shortly after my arrival in Canada five months before—explaining to Canadians how the United States regarded the changing world and how it regarded Canada's place in that new world. The main point of my message was that Canada had to pay greater heed to military preparedness, that there had to be a far greater concern for continental security. I believed in that message, but I had not expected my warning to be proven so right, so fast. In the beautiful heart of Western Canada, the furthest thing from my mind on that morning was terrorism. My wife, Jan, and I were being driven in an RCMP minivan with our consul-general, Roy Chavera, to the Calgary airport for an early morning flight back to Ottawa. Roy's phone rang. It was Roy's wife, Gilda, calling to say a plane had crashed into the World Trade Center. Like most people, I thought at first that this was a terrible accident, a pilot who had suffered a heart attack at the controls, or some similar disaster. But by the time we reached the airport it was clear that this was no accident. Like hundreds of other stunned travelers, we watched on televisions in the airport lounge as a second plane crashed into the World Trade Center and the whole disastrous scenario began to unfold.

Before long came the announcement that all airports in the US had been shut down by the Federal Aviation Administration. We boarded our plane to Ottawa, but within minutes that flight was also canceled. The best we could do was to return to the Calgary consulate where we could at least be in easy contact with the embassy in Ottawa and the State Department in Washington. In the meantime, hundreds of flights on their way to the United States were barred from landing because of the FAA's order. Most of those flights and about 25,000 passengers were rerouted northward to Canadian destinations. When President George W. Bush called Prime Minister Jean Chrétien that morning to ask for Canada's help, our northern neighbor reacted as a true friend does.

For me, being grounded in Calgary at a time like that was incredibly frustrating. Continental air traffic had come to a standstill. Movement at all border crossings between Canada and the United States ground to a crawl. Across the continent—and throughout the world—people were riveted to their televisions screens, trying to come to grips with what was happening. I knew that the embassy staff was up to the challenge of dealing with what was undoubtedly the biggest crisis any of them had ever faced. But I also knew that as ambassador I should be there at the embassy. Since all flights were grounded this seemed impossible.

Within minutes of the attacks, Prime Minister Chrétien had phoned the embassy. He spoke to Stephen Kelly, our deputy chief of mission, and offered to do whatever was needed. He also personally helped Jan and me. The PM dispatched a Canadian Forces Challenger jet to fly us back to Ottawa. It was the eeriest flight we have ever taken. There was none of the usual bustle and noise in the airport. The only activity on the tarmac was the Challenger; it rose smoothly into the 2,000 miles of empty sky that stretched between Calgary and Ottawa.

The city of Ottawa began its life as a raw and crude lumbering town, but over the years it has become one of the world's most beautiful national capitals. Even in those early days of my time in Ottawa the drive in from the airport along the majestic Rideau Canal had come to be something I always looked forward to after a trip—a charming interlude in an otherwise hectic day. Not on that day. Even the Rideau Canal could not lift my spirits or provide a diversion from the heavy thoughts that weighed on my mind.

Like everyone else I was waiting to see what would happen next. Like Americans everywhere, I was waiting for the response of President Bush. His television address on September 13, I think, brought a sense that shock and anger had been joined by a determination to act. His message was clear: The United States of America would find those who attacked us and we would punish them, and we Americans would maintain our way of life and our freedom. This was a test of the resolve not only of the United States but of the peoples throughout the world who were committed to freedom. It was a test, the president said, that we would pass. As world leaders expressed their condemnation of the terrorists who perpetrated the hijackings and mass murders, I saw that there was a determination among the world's democracies to come together and maintain our free and open societies. In France, President Jacques Chirac put it eloquently: "Nous sommes tous Américains"—we are all Americans. Prime Minister Chrétien delivered his own clear promise of support: "Do not despair. You are not alone. We are with you. The whole world is with you.... And together, with our allies, we will defy and defeat the threat that terrorism poses to all civilized nations."

Ordinary Canadians quickly echoed his words. Hundreds left flowers, candles and messages of support at the gates of the US embassy. Like President Chirac, one message evoked the rallying cry of President John F. Kennedy to the embattled people of Berlin when he told them, "Ich bin ein Berliner." That note at the embassy gate from a sympathetic Canadian said simply, "I am an American."

I knew that we could not take Canada's support for granted, but I was confident that Canada would be our partner in the battle against terrorism. Our shared history and values gave me confidence and hope because I knew that we were family. And the Canadian who left the message that "I am an American" believed this too.

Those messages of support were gratifying and inspiring, but I confess that I was not prepared for the demonstration of solidarity on Parliament Hill on September 14. Prime Minister Chrétien had declared a national day of mourning and announced there would be a ceremony at noon that day, a Friday. It was a perfect late summer day, warm and sunny, with clear blue skies—a day that in its beauty was a stunning contrast to the dark events of three days before. Jan and I arrived by car at the rear entrance of the Parliament Buildings. There we met the prime minister and Aline Chrétien, and Governor General Adrienne Clarkson and her husband, John Ralston Saul. We had all arrived by the back entrance because there was an expectation of a large crowd on the front lawns, perhaps as many as 15,000 or even 20,000 people.

Instead there were 100,000 people. They were packed onto the vast lawns of Parliament Hill, they filled Wellington Street that runs across the front of the Hill, and beyond that they thronged Confederation Square and the approaching streets. When we stepped out of the massive doors of the Centre Block, under the magnificent Peace Tower, we were stunned by the sea of people, by the vista of waving American and Canadian flags. The sound of 100,000 people singing the Canadian and American anthems was something I will never forget. At our seats and in the large crowd there were many tears.

The governor general and the prime minister both spoke movingly, expressing the deep sympathy that Canadians felt for the victims and survivors of the terrorist attacks and the outrage that Canadians shared with their American neighbors. In the fight against the kind of barbarism that the world witnessed on September 11, Mr. Chrétien said, the United States could count on Canada.

When my turn to speak came, I faced a daunting task. Not only was there the vast crowd I could see in front of me, but there were hundreds of thousands who would be watching the ceremony on television. I had prepared my speech the day before but I delivered it without notes, struggling with my emotions as I spoke:

> Mister Prime Minister, thank you for your very strong words. These have been tough, tough days for the United States of America and on this beautiful day in Ottawa, such sadness, such beauty. On behalf of President Bush and the people of the United States, I want to thank the Governor General, the Prime Minister and his government, and the people of Canada for your overwhelming support and sympathy.
>
> From accepting and aiding over 25,000 diverted air passengers, to the increased security and protection at our embassy and consulates, to your support at NATO, to the offers, extraordinary offers of assistance, to New York City and Washington DC, to the countless notes of condolence, cards from young children, the flowers and the candles left at our embassy and our consulates across Canada, to this amazing and overwhelming support today here at the capital, you truly are our closest friend.
>
> We will need your continued support and help in the days, and the weeks and the months ahead. The United States and Canada are free and open societies, democracies that respect individual liberty and human rights, and our way of life will be maintained.

The United States and Canada and the freedom-loving nations of this world will win this war against terrorism. And as President Bush has stated, this is a monumental struggle of good versus evil, but good will prevail.

The United States and Canada have an extraordinary friendship, an extraordinary partnership, an extraordinary history of working together. These past few days have reminded me, and, I know, every single citizen of the United States, of what a great friend we have. Thank you.

Just as the events of September 11 and the war on terrorism became the defining struggle of President George W. Bush's first term, so they defined the years when I was privileged to be my country's ambassador in Canada. There were some old familiar problems like the softwood lumber dispute between the two countries, and others of newer vintage like the Canadian government's proposal to decriminalize marijuana possession. But it was the concern about security that was pushed to the top of the American political agenda by September 11, and that concern would set the tone for the next four years at our embassy.

"Security trumps trade" was the message that I would deliver over and over again. Not everyone wanted to hear that message, and to this day I know there are Canadians who are skeptical. But the essence of my view of public diplomacy is that Canadians deserve to be told the plain truth about my government's view of the world and of the issues between us. When you are family, that is how you show respect.

CHAPTER ONE

Small Town Roots

I t is an old curse that condemns you to "live in interesting times." But it was my privilege and good fortune to have four years in Ottawa that were interesting and challenging beyond my imagination. When I arrived in Ottawa in April 2001, I had no idea how challenging it would be, and over those four years I ended up on the front pages of Canadian newspapers on a regular basis. I became the only US ambassador to become the target of a petition demanding that the Canadian government send him home. I even made a guest appearance on CBC Television's frequently manic *This Hour Has 22 Minutes*. Interesting, indeed.

Obviously all this attention was not really about me. I was just the lightning rod that attracted everything that had to do with the Canada–United States relationship. And everything hit the lightning rod, from broad Canadian attitudes toward America to particular attitudes about the president under whom I served, from the relatively small frictions of world politics at any particular moment to the evolving policy of the United States as the world's only superpower. Sooner or later it seemed to hit the Cellucci lightning rod. My job was to explain the policies and goals of the United States government to the Canadian government and to the Canadian people, and inevitably feathers sometimes got ruffled. Others might have chosen to follow a more conventionally "diplomatic" approach, but that was not my personal style and it was not how I conceived "public diplomacy." We had to deal with some very tough issues—the war on terror, and President Bush's decision to invade Iraq, to name only two—and many of those issues were unpopular with some Canadians. Very unpopular. That made my task challenging, but that made the task all that more necessary. After all, that was what public diplomacy was all about. For my efforts, I earned both admiration and enmity. Some called me "straight-spoken" and others described me as "Bush's thug in Canada." One Vancouver columnist even called me Rambo Cellucci. That made my day. But the bottom line is that anyone who knows me and who worked with me during my four years in Canada can affirm that I have nothing but affection and respect for Canadians and their great country. They understand that being candid and upfront is part of the job, and I strongly believe that is the best way to show respect to a friend.

The events of recent years have changed the world and have certainly transformed the context of Canada–United States relations. Even before the events of September 11, 2001, I was talking to Canadians about the desirability of more integration between our two countries on a number of fronts. The American government believed, and we still believe, that even closer cooperation on trade, energy and military matters is in the best interests of both of our countries. September 11 injected greater urgency into that agenda of cooperation and sharply elevated the importance of the security of the American homeland. What would have been eventful and important years in the Canada–United States relationship anyway became ones that I think historians will look back on as transformative.

It was my good fortune to be the American ambassador to Canada during those crucial years, but it was not blind chance. I had asked President George W. Bush for the Ottawa posting. I was completing four years as governor of Massachusetts and 31 consecutive years as an elected official, so it was time for a change. I had worked hard on the president's 2000 campaign, as I had on campaigns for his father going back to 1980. The younger Bush and I were governors of our respective states at the same time; we shared similar political views and we were friends. So I was not shy about volunteering my services for his new administration, and not shy in suggesting in particular that I would like to go to Ottawa. His immediate reaction was to warn me that being ambassador to Canada would be a tough job. The toughness did not bother me, but I would not know my fate until Inauguration Day. At the inaugural parade the president called me down to the front of the reviewing stand—while the assembled governors and senior officials from across the country watched—and quietly told me that he was going to nominate me to be the United States ambassador to Canada. George Tenet, the director of the CIA, was sitting next to Jan. When the president was finished talking Tenet said to Jan, "Something just happened."

What Tenet did not know was that I already knew what Jan's reaction would be. In fact, it was Jan who had suggested that I seek the Ottawa post. We had been to Canada together on several occasions over the years, and she thought the post would be a great challenge for me on the international stage and a natural transition from being a New England governor. Yet neither of us could have imagined how attached we would become to the country that would be our home for the next four years. Nor could we have imagined that it would be a time of some of the most important and emotional moments of our lives. Above all, of course, there was that extraordinary scene on the front lawns of the Parliament Buildings, with 100,000 people singing the American national anthem. Of a much more personal nature was the marriage of our youngest daughter Anne to Calgarian Craig Adams in Ottawa's Notre Dame Cathedral.

There were many, many other events and encounters that made our Canadian years a significant chapter in our lives. Our travels took us north to Alert, south to Pelee Island, from St. John's in the east to Beaver Creek in the west. I don't believe there are many people who have visited all the communities at the extremes of Canada. Along the way we met and talked with thousands of Canadians, and as we went we acquired an enormous love and respect for the country.

Despite those jibes about "Bush's thug" and Rambo Cellucci, Jan often tells people that I was temperamentally suited to the job of ambassador because I am by nature respectful to others. "Respectful" is how Canadians quite rightly think of themselves, but I know that is not the first word that comes to mind when most Canadians think of me and my role as ambassador. The fact is that I think many of my core values are shared by most Canadians—although that may seem hard to believe for those who think of me only in terms of my public persona. That persona is easily described: personal friend of President George W. Bush and the Bush family, former governor of Massachusetts, longtime politician, unusually forthright and outspoken. All of this is true. But there is more to the man than that brief sketch of a public persona; there is a history of who he is and where he comes from that also helps to explain what was said, and the way it was said in those four years in Ottawa, and that history will help to explain my deep respect and genuine admiration for my own country's closest friend.

The first Cellucci in the public life of Hudson, Massachusetts, was my grandfather, Argeo Cellucci, but he spent a long time as a businessman before he succumbed to the call of politics. He was always a busy man, running the family auto dealership that he started in 1920. Those were the days when the automobile was the cutting edge of technology and culture. Everyone wanted to own a car and my grandfather got in on the ground floor. He established the local Oldsmobile franchise in 1923 and for the next 70 years my family sold Oldsmobiles. He was the man the people of Hudson went to when they wanted to become part of the American dream.

Getting elected to the Hudson Public Works Commission in 1958 was a natural step for someone like my grandfather. Everyone knew him and he knew everyone. Selling cars to his neighbors and participating in local politics was in some ways all the same thing. It was about being involved in the life of his community. He won that first election and was re-elected five times. I still remember going door to door in my hometown in 1958, passing out my grandfather's campaign brochures. I was ten years old and I already knew that I loved politics.

My grandfather was proud of what America had done for him and his family, so in 1946, when he returned to his home village in Italy for the first time, he took with him his Oldsmobile 98 convertible. He always drove a 98 convertible. My grandfather wanted his family and village to see with their own eyes and be able to touch that Oldsmobile, the steel and glass symbol of the American Dream. Unfortunately, in those days the roads around my grandfather's village, San Donato, which is east of Rome, were not big enough for that big 98! He had to park the gleaming Olds at the side of the road and walk the final stretch to San Donato. But that was my grandfather, proud of his Italian heritage and grateful to America for the opportunities it gave him and his family.

That visit to Italy re-established the ties to our Italian family and we've remained close ever since. Almost every year someone from our side goes to Italy or Italian family members come to the United States. Over a dozen of my cousins made the trip from Italy to my inauguration as governor in January 1999. My cousin Ornella Cellucci Palieri and her family traveled with us in Canada for two weeks in 2002. And Anne's cousin Susanna Cellucci attended her wedding in Ottawa.

If the Cellucci involvement in politics and public service began with my grandfather, it was my father, Argeo Cellucci Jr. — "Junior," as everyone called him — who was the best politician in the family. He never ran for public office, but no one left a bigger imprint on Hudson than my father. "The man who remade Hudson" is how a local journalist referred to him a few years before his death in 2003. No one who knew my father would dispute that claim.

In my father's high school yearbook he was described as the "most typical Hudsonite," and he was always proud of that. My father shared that sense of place. After he graduated from high school in 1940, he studied at Boston University and went to North Africa with the US Army Air Corps during World War II. But after the war, he returned to Hudson and ran the family car business until he sold it in 1992. He too had the Cellucci sense of home and community. Hudson was his home, the place where he would raise his family and make his life.

Hudson is an old mill town on the Assabet River, about 30 miles west of Boston. By the 1960s, most of the mills had closed and the town's industrial base needed to be redeveloped. My dad was the driving force behind the creation of the Hudson Economic Development Commission in 1963, becoming one of its founding members. For the next 40 years he would act as its chair. He used to say that when the EDC started to sell Hudson as a place for businesses to locate, there were about 15 companies in the town. Forty years later there was 10 times that number, including high-tech companies like Intel. My dad said that every time he brought a new company to town it felt like a personal victory. He was helping transform Hudson into a thriving and prosperous place. The road connecting Hudson to the main interstate is even named after him. Whenever people mention the Cellucci highway they are paying respect to my father's legacy. My father loved the personal side of putting together a package that would bring a new business to town. For him it was an extension of what he had been doing from the time he graduated from Hudson High—selling cars. Someone asked him the secret of his success as chair of the EDC. My father's answer was typically straightforward. "I sell Hudson like I sell Oldsmobiles," he said. "When I brought in Digital Equipment there were no realtors. It was me and one of their vice presidents. We were the two who put it together."

There was another side to my father's involvement in politics that Paul Sullivan, a journalist for the *Sun* newspaper in nearby Lowell, summed up when he called my father "the prince of the powerless." People in town knew that if they had a problem with red tape or they just didn't know where to turn to get something done, that Junior Cellucci was there for them. Until the end of this life he was going to bat for what some would call the little guy, whose state tax refund hadn't arrived or whose daughter needed some medical treatment but couldn't get on a waiting list. Believe me, I know. During the years when I was lieutenant governor and then governor, my father would drive to the capitol every week, sometimes day after day, to press someone's case or to lobby in his capacity as chair of Hudson's EDC. I know that some of my staff would keep their heads down if they knew he was in the building, because my father wouldn't let up until he had a solution to whatever problem he had taken on. He was relentless. But it was always on behalf of someone else or the town.

What I will always remember most about my father is that he led by example, he worked hard, he supported his family and he gave back to his community. You see that and you learn from it. His life was an inspiration for me. When he died, Massachusetts Governor Mitt Romney issued a statement of condolence: "Junior Cellucci brought a tremendous amount of energy and passion to advocating for the needs of his community of Hudson and the Central Massachusetts region." My father never aspired to a higher legacy than that.

He is best remembered for helping people, which he did his entire life, and supporting his family in every way he knew how. At his funeral, my daughter Kate, the first of his grandchildren, told a story that really captured the sort of relationship that he had with the younger generation of Celluccis. Kate explained that she had talked to all of the grandchildren and she found that they were all individually convinced that they were their grandfather's favorite. We all smiled when she said this, because it captured so perfectly the precious and special relationship that my dad had with each of his children and grandchildren.

I was fortunate to grow up in a wonderful family; my immediate and extended family all got along well. I worked closely with my father and grandfather. My mother, Priscilla, instilled in me a very good sense of right and wrong, and she and my father supported me in every endeavor. I was the middle child, my sister, Roseann, being the oldest and my brother, Peter, the youngest.

My sister is now a lawyer in Connecticut, after being a legal librarian for many years. She works with indigent families, a job well suited to the compassionate person that she is. She has an unshakeable faith and is a genuinely caring person. I can attest to the fact that she is also politically savvy. Roseann worked on my 1998 campaign for governor and was a tremendous help, reaching out to various constituencies all across Massachusetts. However, I remember clearly that her first few days on the job were rocky. She was convinced that someone on my campaign staff resented a close family member being on board. The evidence was that every day she would arrive at the campaign head-quarters with a coffee and donut that she put on her desk while she went to hang up her coat. Every day when she got back to her desk her donut was gone. Finally, her fourth day on the job, she put down her donut and coffee and watched from a distance. Sure enough, she spotted the thief and the theft. The thief was Lucy, my campaign manager, Rob Gray's dog. After that the politics was easy.

My brother, Peter, worked in the family automobile business for years and stayed in the industry after my dad sold the dealership in 1992. He and I share a passion for horse racing and golf and we are quite competitive. I wish I could say I always picked more winners and that I always got a lower score in golf, but then I wouldn't be telling the truth. Peter also was an elected member of the Hudson Planning Board for more than a dozen years, and in that position he was able to work closely with my dad on Hudson's economic growth

There is one occasion each year when all the Celluccis get together—Christmas Eve. The celebration has moved from my grandfather's home to my Aunt Helen Rossi's home and now to my home. It happens every year and is, I suppose, a fairly typical Italian-American Christmas get-together. Lots of people, lots of food, lots of noise and lots of affection.

The core of my life for more than 35 years has been my wife Jan. We were high school sweethearts and we have been side by side ever since. In both personal life and political life she keeps me grounded, and when there are difficult times or difficult decisions to be made her unwavering love and support are always there. Only she knows how much I owe her for whatever successes I've had, and for all our years together we have had a confident and happy partnership.

Jan graduated from Regis College in Weston, Massachusetts. She spent her junior year abroad in the historic English city of Bath, where I visited her in the spring of 1971 for three weeks. We saw some of the sights in London and then headed off to the Greek island of Corfu. Two college kids in Corfu, where the blue sky and white houses are more beautiful than any postcard can convey; it was unforgettable. From there we went to Italy to visit my grandfather, who happened to be visiting our Italian relatives.

It was an idyllic trip with only one small glitch. On the day that I left for Europe my first-year torts professor at Boston College, Professor Jim Smith, had called upon me to answer a question. When he saw that I wasn't there, he asked whether anyone knew where Cellucci was. My friend Jerry Bruen, instead of telling Professor Smith that I was sick or stuck in traffic, told him that I had gone to Europe for three weeks. When I returned to class, Professor Smith was waiting for me. "Mr. Cellucci, how was your trip to Europe?" I guess I had already acquired an important political skill, the ability not to be put off stride by an unexpected question. "Great," I answered, "I wish I was still there." Professor Smith then spent the rest of the class firing question after question at me in the Socratic style. I somehow survived it and I'm sure it was good training for the grilling that I would sometimes get during my years in politics.

The final chapter of our idyllic trip to Europe together was written back in America. Jan returned to dorm life in Massachusetts after living in a beautiful apartment in Bath. After her first night back at Regis College she told me, "I don't like living in the dormitory," so I said, "Let's get married." She said yes. Jan's parents, Alice and Ed Garnett, were close friends of my parents, and we all met a few days later in my parents' den to begin planning our wedding. Two months later, on November 12, 1971, we were married in the chapel at Regis College. Asking Jan to marry me was by far the best thing I've ever done.

After Jan graduated from Regis College she went on to get her master's degree in library science from Simmons College in Boston. Her career started at the Hudson public library, moving on to become an elementary school library media specialist with the Hudson public schools. Jan took some time out to be at home with Kate and Anne when they were young, but even then she continued in her professional career. With the help of the vaunted Cellucci political machine, Jan was elected to two terms as a member of the Hudson Board of Library Trustees. Another Cellucci in politics!

When our girls started school, Jan followed them, working as a library volunteer at the St. Michael's Grammar School in Hudson. When our daughters changed schools, Jan went with them, becoming the children's librarian and then the library director at the Bancroft School, an independent K–12 day school in Worcester, Massachusetts where Kate and Anne attended middle and upper school. After several years there, Jan became the preservation manager for the Boston College Libraries, where Kate was enrolled, and then was promoted to the position of associate university librarian for collection services.

During our years in Canada, Jan was able to draw on this experience and the passion that she has for her profession, visiting more than thirty libraries and archives across the country to promote their services and resources to Canadian decision-makers. She is an enthusiastic and articulate advocate of all that libraries and archives do to preserve the past and make it a living resource for the present. While in Canada, Jan became a member of the University of British Columbia President's Advisory Council on the University Library. She also joined the Strategic Planning Committee of the Friends of

Library and Archives Canada. While in Ottawa, Jan was the assistant curator of the "On the Road/Sur la route" rare books exhibit at Library and Archives Canada. And I am proud to say that it was Jan's idea to take the President and Mrs. Bush to the Library and Archives Canada's Preservation Centre in Gatineau, Quebec, when they visited in November 2004. Jan introduced them there to the breadth and depth of our two nations' shared heritage. The president and first lady loved it.

Jan and I are blessed with two wonderful daughters, and I'm very proud of both of them. Kate, the oldest, left a promising accounting career to become a grade 7 science teacher. She had graduated from the Boston College School of Management as one of top students in her accounting class, but after working for Deloitte & Touche for a year, she decided to go back to university to get a master's degree in education. She really connects with the children she teaches. I visit her classroom every year to meet her students. In my final State of the State address as governor, delivered at historic Mechanics Hall in Worcester, while talking about the importance of teaching, I was proud to tell the people of Massachusetts that my daughter Kate had become a teacher. Kate continues the Cellucci tradition of public service in our hometown.

Anne, my youngest daughter, works in the entertainment industry between her travels with her husband, Craig, an NHL hockey player. After graduating from Harvard, Anne worked as a production assistant for the film *Ocean's Eleven*, produced by a Bush family friend, Jerry Weintraub. In the NHL off-season Anne works at Pyramid Productions in Calgary, a leading Canadian film and television production studio. When the players were locked out for the 2004–05 season, Anne and Craig decided to go to Italy where Craig played in Milan. While Craig played hockey, Anne learned Italian, a language that she had always wanted to learn so that she could communicate better with our Italian family. Jan and I were delighted when after just six months of living in Italy, Anne was speaking Italian fluently with her cousins and guiding us knowledgeably through Milan and Venice.

I'm also proud of my son-in-law. He and Anne met when they were both attending Harvard University. Craig was captain of the hockey team during his senior year. Although he was raised in Calgary, Craig was born in Brunei when his parents, Mike and Hilary Adams, were living there. Craig's dad was working for Shell Oil and Brunei is a small island country whose wealth is based on its significant petroleum reserves. Jan and I are delighted to have this permanent family connection to Canada, including the distinction of having a son-in-law who is the only NHLer from Brunei. Each year during our time in Ottawa I would attend the Brunei National Day celebration and proudly tell the high commissioner, Serbinia Ali, that my son-in-law was born in his country. I don't think he had run into many people in Canada who had family connections to Brunei. Craig's family memeburs have become our closest friends in Canada. Mike is a petroleum engineer, and Hilary is a family physician. Craig's brother Gareth is an exercise physiologist. Jan and I expect to travel to Calgary often to be with them.

Craig had already played four seasons for the Carolina Hurricanes in the NHL before going to play in Italy during the lockout. His team, the Milano Vipers, finished first in the regular season and won the league championship in the playoffs.

I was still in college when I was elected to the Hudson Charter Commission. I was all of 21 years old, which was voting age at the time. The first person I ever voted for was myself. The Charter Commission wrote a new charter, a constitution for local government, for Hudson. A year later the voters adopted the new Charter, which among other things increased the membership of the Board of Selectmen, the political body that in New England towns serves in the place of mayors. Naturally, I ran for one of the new seats. I won that election, the first of two three-year terms on the Hudson Board of Selectmen. I really got my start in politics on the ground floor, where you learn about keeping in touch with the day-to-day concerns of the people you represent. I ran for the state House of Representatives in 1976 and for the next 24 years I worked at the State House in Boston, as a member of the state House of Representatives, and at the state Senate, then as lieutenant governor and finally as governor of Massachusetts.

That's a lot of years in politics and a lot of elections. In fact, from my first campaign for the Hudson Charter Commission to my run for the governor in 1998, I campaigned in 13 elections. I won every one of them. Jan always thought that each election would be the last, but the voters kept on electing me. Her natural irreverence and skepticism about what motivates politicians have always provided a good balance to my earnest approach. If I had lost, I would have moved on with our life and I would have devoted more time to my law practice and to business. Thirteen election campaigns is a lot to ask of even the most supportive spouse—and Jan was certainly that, although maybe there were times when she might have been just as happy to see me sit one out. But Jan always gave me her blessing to go for it again—or at least that's what I thought I heard.

When I started to think about getting involved in state politics I didn't feel any family pressure to join one party or the other. But there were many reasons why I thought the Republican Party made sense for me, although Massachusetts is a very Democratic state. In general, my ideas about politics and economics were much more in tune with those of the Republican Party. I've always been strongly pro-business, believing that less regulation and lower taxes was the best way to generate jobs for people. My father and grandfather were also Republicans. Growing up in what was then a lower-middle-class town I saw people working hard to provide their children with more education and better opportunities. Government spending and taxes were growing, but my neighbors' ability to pay for their groceries, college tuition, mortgages and all the rest of the things that squeeze every last dime out of an ordinary family's pocketbook weren't growing nearly as fast. Some people think that growing up in a community of working people, many of them first- and second-generation Americans from Italy and Portugal, with lots of people of Irish ancestry in the demographic mix, it would have been natural to become a Democrat. That's not how I saw it. Instead I saw people whose lives and opportunities were more likely to be improved by lower taxation and less government, not more. I've always been a fiscal conservative, so the Republican Party was a natural home for me. I cut taxes more than any governor in our state's history. I believe I put a stake in the heart of that old label "Taxachusetts." I also insisted on higher standards in the classroom so that our students would have the necessary skills to compete in today's world. But I wouldn't call myself a social conservative. In the northeast the Republican Party has long been less conservative on many social questions than Republicans in the South and parts of the Midwest.

Ideas and policy aside, the other reason why I threw in my lot with the Republican Party was because I felt there were more opportunities for a young person like me. The Massachusetts Republican Party was a lot smaller than the Democratic Party and a good deal less popular. The less popular part wasn't much of an inducement to join, but the prospect of being able to win the party's nomination for my district looked promising and the prospects of advancing in the party were also good. My conviction was that retail politics — going door-to-door, person-to-person, meeting small groups and shaking hands outside factory gates and at malls — was important in my part of the state. As it turned out I was right. I won seven consecutive elections for the state House and Senate.

In my first campaign for the state House of Representatives in 1976, I pledged that I would ring every doorbell in the district. I started on a swelteringly hot July day and for the next four months, four hours each day, taking only Sundays off, I rang the bell and knocked on about 7,000 doors. But there are occupational hazards to door-to-door campaigning. Although I was unopposed in the Republican primary, even on primary election day I was out knocking on doors. On the last street of the night I was treated quite well, invited in for pasta at one home and for dessert at another. But at the final house of the day, the home of a man whose daughter was a client of mine at my law office, their little dog ran out the door and bit me in the leg, drawing blood. This was my third dog bite of that campaign. Like a postman, you come to think of it as something that comes with the turf. So I went to the hospital to get a tetanus shot. Later that evening I went to the Hudson town hall to find out who my Democratic opponent would be. While I was waiting for the results of the Democratic primary to come in I was chatting with a local reporter and told him about my run-in with the dog earlier that evening.

The next morning the local radio station reported that I had received a shot in the arm. There were different reactions to the news. When my law partner, Jack Kittredge, went to Kelly Diorio's barber shop later that morning, he bumped into Manuel Machado an elderly Portuguese gentleman who said to him in broken English, "Tell the kid to get some dog biscuits." Rather practical advice. A different reaction greeted Jan when she arrived at school that day. One of the little girls ran up to her and said, "I loved him, too." Apparently she had heard that I had received a shot, but not about the dog bite, and she feared my wound had been a bullet. Politics can be dangerous, but I'm pleased to report that the worst shot that I ever received came from a doctor's needle.

In politics you get called all sorts of names and I've been on the receiving end of a lot of them during my lifetime. One of them is "career politician." Despite having worked for my family's automobile business and having had a law practice for all my years in the state legislature, there were people who tried to brand me a political careerist. From the mouths and pens of some people this was intended to sting. But I've never let it bother me and apparently it didn't bother the people who voted for me over the years.

During my entire political career in Massachusetts I lived in Hudson, including the time I was governor. Massachusetts is one of only five states that don't have an official residence for the governor, something that goes back to the American Revolution and the rejection of any trappings of royalty and privilege. So even during my years as governor I would still be driven home each day to Hudson. People would see me on weekends having dinner at Bertucci's with Joe and Judy Hart, visiting my best friend, Bob Yesue, at his barber shop and hair salon, meeting my dad at Nick's Diner, grocery shopping or mowing my lawn. I was probably the only governor in the United States who did the family grocery shopping and cut his own grass.

The result, of course, was that there were lots of times when people who had known me for years, sometimes from the time I was a young boy, would come up to me at a restaurant or a store and let me know in clear terms what they thought I was doing wrong or doing right. Whatever else they may have thought of me, at least they did not regard me as a distant and unapproachable career politician. I was part of the community. I was their neighbor.

CHAPTER TWO

From the State House to the Ambassador's House

The road that carried me to Ottawa in the early spring of 2001 had begun two decades earlier, and that road was rooted profoundly in the politics and personalities of Massachusetts. At the time, I was a second-term member of the Massachusetts House of Representatives. For Republicans the late 1970s not an auspicious time. There was a grand total of 30 in the Republican caucus, compared to 130 Democrats, and another 6 Republicans among the 40 state senators. The governor, Edward King, was a Democrat and Democrats controlled most of the state legislatures and governorships across the country. In Washington the Democrats had sizeable majorities in both the House and the Senate and the president, Jimmy Carter, was a Democrat. As I said, not a great time for Republicans; there seemed to be Democrats everywhere.

However, when the candidates for the Republican Party's presidential nomination started to get serious about raising money and preparing for the primaries, I knew that the 1980 election would be important for us. I also believed that it was an election that we could win. The economy was sputtering and President Carter was not having much success getting his legislative agenda through Congress. I thought that our prospects of recapturing the White House looked promising.

What I didn't know was who I would support for the Republican nomination. There were several candidates, with Ronald Reagan regarded as the frontrunner. I received a phone call from my friend David Sparks who was helping George H.W. Bush of Texas. I'd read about Bush and was impressed with his experience. I asked David to tell me more about him, which he did. As he talked I made an instinctive and instant decision that would set the course for my political life for at least the next quarter century. Impulsively I told David to tell George Bush that I was with him.

I had an intuitive sense at the time that George Bush was the right candidate for the party. As it happened, the majority of the Republican Party did not agree with me. The party's choice was Ronald Reagan, but my consolation was that he chose George Bush as his running mate. It wasn't that I didn't like Reagan or, for that matter, the other candidates; in fact I worked hard on the Reagan presidential campaign after he won the Republican nomination. But I just had a good feeling about George Bush and the values and policies he stood for. Still, things turned out well in the end. Ronald Reagan recaptured the White House and played the leading role in improving the Republicans' election prospects across the country. George Bush became his vice-president and then won the presidency in 1988 against Michael Dukakis, the Democratic governor of my state.

If those days got me hooked on national politics, they also threw me into the company of people who were destined to be my close colleagues and friends for a long time to come. I remember the first time I met George Bush. It was in September, 1979, in a downtown Boston hotel, and I introduced him to Andy Card, Andrew Natsios,

Leon Lombardi and several other colleagues from the Massachusetts House of Representatives. We all liked George Bush. He connected with us. There he was, running for president of the United States, but he was still interested in what we were doing in the Massachusetts legislature. His interest impressed us, and the four of us became the co-chairs of the Bush campaign in our state. He called us his "Four Horsemen." He described us as state legislators who voted with our hearts, although, he said, we were always mindful of the taxpayer's pocketbook.

That 1980 campaign gave me the chance to get to know George Bush. I drove him from campaign stop to campaign stop in an Oldsmobile Vista Cruiser from my family's dealership. We logged a lot of miles and drank a lot of coffee as we crisscrossed the state stumping for votes.

Memory stores away odd fragments. I remember, in the middle of that campaign, being in Worcester and leaving Channel 27 after an interview. George Bush got a coffee and climbed into the car next to me. As we started to pull away he said, "Stop the car." We stopped and he opened his door and carefully poured out some of the hot coffee to make it a bit easier to handle as we drove. Ten years later when I picked up Bill Weld at his Cambridge home for a day of campaigning, he came out with a hot coffee. As we pulled away from his house he asked me to stop, and he opened the door and poured out some of his coffee so that it wouldn't spill. I had a premonition of good things for the Weld–Cellucci partnership. It turned out that I was right.

Bush had the momentum coming out of the 1980 Iowa caucuses. But in New Hampshire, after a good performance in the primary debate with Bush, Ronald Reagan started his comeback and scored a big win. As the first primary in the nation, New Hampshire is critical in determining who eventually wins the party presidential nomination. The Boston media market overlaps southern New Hampshire, and Massachusetts political people always play a big role in the New Hampshire primaries. Bush had spent a lot of time in the Granite State, so we were disappointed with the result. But we didn't have time to brood over what was past. The Massachusetts primary would be in a week.

The race for the Republican nomination was down to three candidates—George Bush, Ronald Reagan and Illinois Congressman John Anderson. Along with the rest of the Bush campaign team, I was working flat out. I'm pleased to record that the 14 speeches that I made in a single day was the record for the campaign. Finally, at 4:00 a.m. in the Statler Hotel in Boston, with Jim Baker in our campaign war room, we cheered as George Bush went over the top to win the Massachusetts primary. That win did not get him the presidential nomination, but I like to think that his victory was an important factor in Bush being able to stay in the 1980 primary race and eventually being selected as Ronald Reagan's running mate. It was heady time for the Four Horsemen.

Our early meeting with Bush was particularly significant for Andy Card. He would eventually go on to work in the White House for Ronald Reagan, George H. W. Bush and George W. Bush. I like to remind him that I was the one who introduced him to George H. W. Bush. Andy has been one of my best friends over the years, and the fact that he was White House chief of staff during my time in Ottawa gave me a pipeline to the president that most ambassadors don't have. While I was in Ottawa I talked to him at least once a week, which means that there has probably been no other period when the presidential chief of staff was as well informed about Canadian affairs.

Andy was born and raised in Holbrook, Massachusetts, about an hour's drive from Hudson. Many people think of him as the most prominent and influential Massachusetts Republican of his generation in national politics, and it would be hard to argue with that assessment. Andy was elected to the Massachusetts state house two years before me. He ran for governor in 1982 with me as his campaign chairman. He didn't win that election, but he was a credible and capable candidate. Andy played a critical role in my 1998 campaign for governor. He became a senior advisor to the campaign with the necessary gravitas to pull everyone together.

After Andy's defeat in the 1982 governor's race, he was offered the job of intergovernmental affairs advisor in the White House, marking the start of his long association with Republican presidents. Most recently, of course, Andy was named President George W. Bush's chief of staff. As gatekeeper to the Oval Office he has a huge influence on who has access to President Bush and on almost all aspects of the president's schedule. Back when we were in the Massachusetts legislature together we used to call Andy the "boy scout." He was such an honest straight shooter that you knew he could always be counted on to do the right thing and to know what the right thing was. Any administration needs someone with his character to help keep the moral compass pointing north. I've always been honored to be able to count him among my best friends.

Andrew Natsios, another friend from my early days in the Massachusetts legislature, is someone whose career has taken him to some of the world's hotspots and most desolate corners. When Natsios first worked for USAID, back in 1990, he was taken prisoner for several hours in southern Sudan by gun–toting guards, his plane narrowly escaped mortar fire in Eritrea, and he was in a car that was hit by gunfire when he was in Sarajevo. He jokes that it was his background in Massachusetts politics that prepared him for the dangers that he faced in places throughout the world—"You fall once, and the wolves are on you, and you're gone."

When I was elected governor in 1998 I turned to Andrew Natsios to become my secretary of administration and finance, the top administrative job in the Massachusetts state government. It was Natsios who first warned me that the "Big Dig"—an enormous project to put the elevated central artery highway in Boston underground—was facing potentially huge cost overruns. It was his persistence and dogged pressure that enabled us to establish what the real costs of this project were likely to be. When I asked him to take on the job of chairman of the Massachusetts Turnpike Authority, with responsibility for the Big Dig project that had by then become national news, he could have said, "No, thanks." But he didn't. Andrew took on a job that placed him squarely at the eye of the storm and he restored fiscal credibility to that important project. Of course, at the time I had to fire Jim Kerasiotes for failing to tell me, federal highway officials, and the people of Massachusetts about these large cost overruns. But I do believe that as Fred Salvucci, Governor Dukakis's Secretary of Transportation, will be remembered as "The Architect of the Big Dig" (it was his idea), that Jim Kerasioties will be remembered as the "The Builder of the Big Dig." I also believe that, despite the huge overruns, the leaks, and the continuing controversy, history will judge this massive construction project as an engineering marvel that unclogged the many bottlenecks in Boston traffic, and resotred the history and stature of my country's most historic city.

But back to Andrew Natsios, as loyal a friend as anyone could have and a man who thrives on challenges that most people would flee from. When President Bush was elected, Andrew returned to the international development work that he loves best. He was chosen to be head of USAID and in that capacity he has been the person most responsible for the job of reconstruction in post-Taliban Afghanistan and Iraq after the fall of Saddam Hussein. Many people don't realize that the United States is the world's largest donor of foreign aid, and Andrew is the person in charge of that multibillion dollar budget. This brings him into contact with leaders throughout the world. But he is still the person I knew almost 30 years ago in the Massachusetts legislature, a compassionate conservative who has always wanted to help improve people's lives.

Leon Lombardi is now a trial judge of the Massachusetts Land Court. He also did a stint as chairman of the Massachusetts Republican Party. Ron Kaufman is another friend and colleague who was with the Bush campaign at the beginning. Ron is one of the best operatives the Republican Party has and was a key advisor in all of my state-wide campaigns.

Our team was also heavily involved in Vice President Bush's 1988 campaign. That campaign brought me even closer to the Bush family, for I was a state Senator and chair of the Bush campaign in Massachusetts. This was significant because Vice President Bush's rival for the presidency was Michael Dukakis, the Democratic governor of my state. Massachusetts is usually a safe Democratic state in presidential general elections. But in 1988 it became one of the focal points in the race in which Vice President Bush was well down in the early national polls.

We were determined to help George Bush win the presidency, even though it meant an open challenge to our own state governor. I would attend press conferences at the state House, listening respectfully to Governor Dukakis; then, when he left the room, I would give the press the other side. We had Vice President Bush visit the Boston Harbor, which was the most polluted in America, to mock the Dukakis campaign's claim to the high ground on environmental issues. And a few weeks later the vice president came back to accept the endorsement of the Boston Police Patrolmen's Association. It was like operating behind enemy lines.

The day Vice President Bush arrived to visit the harbor I met him at Logan Airport with a copy of the *Boston Herald*. The front page story showed that he and Governor Dukakis were in a dead heat in the polls in Massachusetts. Then, just before election day I traveled to Fairfield University in Connecticut, where I handed the vice president another copy of the *Boston Herald*. The headline read, "What a Mess!" The story was about the sorry state of Massachusetts' public finances under Governor Dukakis. Vice President Bush held up the paper at a rally there and in Ohio later that day. It was great fun and important work and in the end the result was a resounding Bush victory.

Those early days of helping George Bush bonded all of us to the Bush family and to each other. I was proud that Andy, Andrew, Leon and Ron all attended my daughter Anne's wedding in the summer of 2003. We all smoked a celebratory cigar that day. Reflecting on where life had taken each of us, we had a lot to celebrate. For me, it was my daughter's wedding and the good fortune that had taken me to Ottawa. For Andy Card, it was the fact that he had risen to become chief-of-staff in the White House. Andrew Natsios was running the Agency for International Development. Leon Lombardi had become a respected judge. And Ron Kaufman was doing very well in the private sector, while continuing to help lead the Republican Party nationally.

In December of 2004, I attended the dedication of a new bocci court in the north end of Boston, named after my father. My good friend Sal DiMasi, Democratic Speaker of the Massachusetts House of Representatives, had shepherded the bill that honored my father through the legislature. At the dedication ceremony were Jan, my sister, Roseann, and my mother, Priscilla, as well as many members of the legislature, some of whom went back to the days when I was a rookie state legislator. In Sal's speech that day he mentioned that many years before in the state legislature, when we would be loudly challenging the Democratic majority, he would lean over and whisper in my ear or in Andy Card's ear or in Andrew Natsios's ear, "You're Republicans in Massachusetts. You'll never amount to anything in politics!" Sal's an astute guy, but I guess we proved him wrong.

We had a bocci match that day, with Governor Mitt Romney and me on the same team. I'm sure that whoever drew up the teams thought that Governor Romney, never having played bocci before, would drag down my team. In fact, though, he turned out to be a very good player and we won. Senator Robert Traviglini, the president of the Massachusetts Senate, was visibly disappointed. He takes his bocci seriously, as do many Italians in Boston. Trav is also a great friend, and a great bocci player.

My personal relationship with President George W. Bush goes back to those early campaigns for his dad. We became even closer, though, when we were governors together. The day after I was elected governor in 1998, he called me from Texas with his congratulations. He was amazed that a Republican had won again in Massachusetts. I told him then that I thought he should run for president and that if he did I was with him all the way. He said, "That's not why I'm calling you," but I know he appreciated my early support.

At the February 1999 National Governors Association meeting in Washington DC, Governor John Engler of Michigan, Governor Marc Racicot of Montana and I got the signal from Governor Bush to round up other Republican governors for his presidential bid. He was not yet an announced candidate, but within 24 hours we managed to get commitments of support from 16 of 31 Republican governors. Eventually all but one Republican governor supported him. This was an important milestone on Governor Bush's road to the White House

In November 1998, I had been part of a week-long trip to Israel with a group that included Governor Bush, Governor Racicot and Governor Leavitt of Utah. We visited all the religious sites, including the Old City, the Wailing Wall and the Church of the Holy Sepulchre. We also went up in an Israeli helicopter with Ariel Sharon, who was minister of national infrastructure at the time under Prime Minister Benjamin Netanyahu. From the air it was easy to see why this region is such a tinderbox—everything is so close and enemies are separated from one another by so little space.

I know that many people were critical of President Bush when he was first elected because they believed he knew little about the world. But the fellow governor I traveled with in Israel was a man who had a strong interest in this troubled part of the globe and who was obviously a fast learner in foreign affairs. He was already receiving briefings on foreign policy from people who would become part of his administration. No one who got to know Governor Bush as I did would have ever made the mistake of underestimating him and his ability to lead the United States through difficult times. I also remember telling my chief of staff, Ginny Buckingham, on my return from Israel that Governor Bush is like his father. Someone had asked him why he might run for president, and he answered: "Duty."

Not surprisingly, I was heavily involved in the 2000 presidential election in support of the younger George Bush. My political team and I took an active role in the campaign in New Hampshire. We sent busloads of fieldworkers to crisscross the state and I personally campaigned long and hard—stealing time from my already busy schedule as governor of Massachusetts. However, once again, New

Hampshire was not Bush country. I remember meeting with the governor in Nashua that evening. He was, naturally, a bit down. I gave him a hug and said, "Hang in there. Better days lie ahead." I suppose that as a Republican in Massachusetts you have to believe that your fortunes are going to improve. It turned out that I was right, though. There were indeed better days ahead.

My Massachusetts political staff traveled the country campaigning for Governor Bush. And when the campaigning was done we sent people to Florida to help in the recount. Our efforts in Massachusetts were fruitless as the state voted solidly for Al Gore, but we raised a lot of money for the Bush campaign. We may not have generated a lot of votes, but we were one of the largest donor states in the Republican presidential campaign. Dick Egan of EMC directed this effort, with help from my top fundraiser, Jim Connolly, and others.

In September 2000, Governor Bush was in Massachusetts for the final presidential debate. I met him at Logan Airport and in the backseat of the car heading to his hotel he asked me, "Do you think Andy Card will be willing to saddle up again?" Andy had managed the Republican presidential convention that summer and was managing the debates for Governor Bush. I knew that the governor was talking about Andy becoming chief of staff in his administration. I said yes, knowing that Andy's strong sense of public service would not let him say no to an offer to serve his third president. Andy had been deputy chief of staff and secretary of transportation under President Bush's father. We didn't talk about what, if any, role I might play in a new Republican administration. I was too absorbed in my job as governor of Massachusetts to think seriously about doing anything else. It may be, though, that after 30 years in state politics the thought of trying my hand at something else, if the right opportunity arose, was simmering somewhere below the surface.

Of course Governor Bush did well in that Boston debate, partly because of Vice President Gore's awful television make-up and his annoying tendency to sigh audibly whenever Governor Bush answered a question. But even more important to Governor Bush's success in that debate was the fact that he is smart and capable, and he showed this to the American people. I never understood the Gore campaign's tactic of trying to convince voters that Governor Bush was not bright enough to be president. Not only was the charge wholly untrue, it also lowered expectations for Governor Bush going into the debates. I've always wanted to ask Vice President Gore, "If George Bush isn't smart, but can best you in debate, what does that make you?"

I spoke with Governor Bush by phone shortly before he was declared the winner of the 2000 election. I told him that I'd like to work for him in his new administration. He replied that we'd have to find something that was good for him and good for me. I said, "I think I have something."

"What's that?"

"I would like to be appointed the United States Ambassador to Canada."

"That's a big job."

"I know it is."

I went on to tell him that as a New England governor I had worked closely with Eastern Canadian premiers and that I knew how important the Canada–United States relationship was. It was a job where I knew I could help his administration. President Bush understood the importance of the relationship. As governor of Texas, he had worked regularly on a range of bilateral issues with Mexico, his state's big neighbor to the south. He was well aware of the significance of NAFTA and of our Canadian and Mexican trading partners.

I saw the president-elect two weeks later at his ranch in Crawford, Texas, where he had invited all the Republican governors for a barbecue and some discussion. In a private moment I reminded him of our conversation about Canada. He said to me, "Don't take silence as a negative." I let the matter rest until the president's inauguration, on January 20, 2001, when he called me over and told me I had the job. Jan and I were excited by this new opportunity.

Even so, the prospect of leaving Hudson and the state that we had called home for all our lives was not easy to accept. Jan loved her job as associate university librarian at Boston College and I loved being governor of Massachusetts. But timing is crucial in politics. I had just succeeded in having a referendum approved on the November 2000 ballot. It brought about the largest tax cut in Massachusetts history. I had led the effort to collect the signatures to get the question on the ballot. I had raised the money to run radio and television ads in support of the proposed tax cut. I had even debated four different Democratic leaders in four televised debates on the issue. This was another state-wide campaign, pretty much like running for re-election. Senator Kennedy, Senator Kerry, all 10 Massachusetts congressmen, most Democrats in the state legislature and most of the labor unions opposed me and the tax cut that I championed. Yet on the same ballot where the voters of Massachusetts favored Al Gore over George W. Bush by a margin of about 30 points, they approved my tax cut 59 percent to 41 percent. This was a major victory for the taxpayers of my state.

I also succeeded in maintaining the state education standards in our schools. These standards, which required that students pass exams in basic math and English to receive a high school diploma, were a major piece of the Education Reform Act of 1993 and were being phased in over time. The teacher unions wanted to weaken the standards just as they were about to take effect. I worked closely with the speaker of the House, Tom Finneran, and Thomas Birmingham, president of the state Senate, both Democrats, to hold the line on this issue. The standards have since taken effect and the results are in: improved educational outcomes for the students of my state.

Although I had been governor for four years, it felt like I was into my third term. As lieutenant governor for six years under Governor Weld, I had been given a lot or responsibility. Weld was a great person to work for. A natural leader, he led Massachusetts out of very difficult times in the early 1990s, and he never worried about who got the credit. I remember one staff meeting in which Governor Weld was advised that a blizzard was coming in; a staff member said he would call the governor at five o'clock the next morning to see whether a state of emergency should be declared. Governor Weld simply looked up and said, "Call Paul." And the next morning at five I did get a call and I did declare a state of emergency—while Governor Weld slept comfortably in his Cambridge home. By January 2001, I was completing my thirty-first year as an elected official in state politics. I knew that if I wanted to be part of the president's administration, I had to seize the opportunity. Once the nominations for cabinet, federal agencies and ambassadorial postings were made and started to grind through the Senate confirmation mill, that window of opportunity would be closed for several years and possibly longer. At the same time, I was proud of what I had accomplished in Massachusetts politics and I knew that I would miss it.

As I looked back over my years of public service, and particularly my time as lieutenant governor and then governor, I felt that some good things had been accomplished for the people and state of Massachusetts. Many people recall that after Governor Dukakis lost his bid for the White House in 1988 he said of the state, "The future's so bright you gotta wear shades." Well, the truth was that after the high-tech–driven "Massachusetts Miracle" of the 1980s, the economy was heading south and the state budget was on course for disaster.

When Bill Weld and I came into office in 1991, the words "cutting taxes" were not part of the legislature's vocabulary. Massachusetts was better known as "Taxachusetts." The state, like the nation, was in a deep recession, but in Massachusetts that recession got even deeper because in the later 1980s the Democrat-dominated legislature tried to tax and spend its way out of a fiscal crisis. We had, in 1991, the highest unemployment rate in America. Our bond rating was ranked dead last among the states, just one notch above junk bond status.

The people of Massachusetts were fed up with having the state's budget books balanced with their tax dollars, and businesses were frustrated with a tax code that discouraged new investment. All of those things led to a strong appetite in Massachusetts for tax cuts. So we rolled up our sleeves and started cutting taxes. We repealed the sales tax on services. We eliminated the tax on long-term capital gains. We put in place one of the most generous research-and-development tax credits in the country. We eliminated the tax on internet access and in the summer of 1998 alone we managed to pass $1 billion in tax cuts. Over a period of 10 years, we passed about 40 tax cuts which helped pump billions of dollars annually into our economy and helped the families of Massachusetts.

But we did something else too: we changed the political debate in Massachusetts. Even liberal Democrats were touting their own tax cut packages. In Massachusetts, that's when you know things have changed. Democrats could no longer ignore the obvious. Tax cuts were working for our economy and our families. We had a thriving high-technology sector and the lowest unemployment rate of the big industrial states. We also had our bond rating significantly upgraded by Wall Street. We had taken the old "Taxachusetts" label and driven a stake through its heart.

I'm probably best remembered for my pro-taxpayer and pro-business policies, but there is another side of my record of which I'm equally proud. My record on social issues was moderate and in tune with voters on Main Street. I supported *Roe v. Wade* and abortion rights, which did not always make me popular with the Catholic Church. In fact Cardinal Bernard Law "disinvited" me from speaking at the commencement of my god-daughter, Heather Yesue, at my alma mater, Hudson Catholic High School. This was the same Cardinal Law who later became the center of extraordinary controversy for his handling of the pedophile scandal in the Boston archdiocese. I have great respect for the Catholic Church and its theology of hope, but I believe that abortion is an intensely personal decision for a woman and that government should not interfere. I took a conservative approach to crime, supporting mandatory minimum sentencing for violent offenders. And in 1998 I signed into law the toughest gun control measure in the United States. My administration also expanded health care coverage to low-income families and to include all children in Massachusetts.

I'm proud too of the fact that I appointed many women to high-ranking positions. I named Margaret H. Marshall as the first female chief justice of the Massachusetts Supreme Judicial Court, the first woman to lead a branch of government in almost 400 years of state history. I appointed Martha Sosman and Judith Cowins to vacancies on the Supreme Judicial Court, which meant that I had appointed more women to the court than all previous Massachusetts governors combined. I was quite surprised when Justice Cowins cast the deciding vote to legalize gay marriage in Massachusetts. My chief legal counsel, Len Lewin, and I had long discussions with each of the potential nominees to the court about the role of the legislature and the people in a democracy. But I do respect the independence of the judiciary and I do believe that the decision of the Massachusetts Supreme Judicial Court on gay marriage made John Kerry's quest for the presidency more difficult. I asked Jane Swift to be my running mate in the 1998 gubernatorial election, and when I left to become ambassador she became the first woman in Massachusetts history to occupy the governor's office. I appointed several women to major administrative positions, including Virginia Buckingham to run the Massachusetts Port Authority. Some men had a problem with all these women that I appointed to important positions, but my message to those who felt threatened by powerful women was blunt: Get a life. I was also quite surprised and very disappointed by Governor Swift's lack of leadership after 9/11 when she played politics and forced Buckingham to step down as CEO of Massport and Logan Airport. But I remain proud of the legacy of diverse appointments I left behind.

The positions that I took on most social issues were ones that I think a majority of Canadians would approve. I was always supportive of equal rights for gays and lesbians, although I am not in favor of changing the legal definition of marriage to include same-sex couples. Conservative-leaning on fiscal matters and moderate on social issues—that's how I would summarize my political philosophy. It helped get me elected governor and possibly has been the key to Republican control of the Massachusetts governorship since the 1990 election. It's a formula that I think many Canadians look for in their own political leaders. When I ran in 1998, I had significant support from labor and the endorsement of more than two dozen Democrats who called themselves "Democrats for Cellucci." Even the Democratic House Speaker, Tom Finneran, and the mayor of Boston, Tom Menino, were perceived by many as preferring me to my Democratic rival for governor.

I've always been a coalition builder in politics, a necessary survival skill when your party is outnumbered four-to-one as mine was during my time in state government. It is important to hold and remain faithful to core principles and strong beliefs, but you also have to respect other views. During my years as United States ambassador to Canada, I was more often portrayed as defiant than conciliatory. I don't deny the defiant side and in many ways I would say that defiant is my best mode. But only when I have to be. Only when this is what the circumstances require. Otherwise my natural tendency is to look for common ground and try to bridge the differences that separate the parties at the table. I would never have survived and succeeded all those years in Massachusetts politics—as a Republican in a liberal-Democrat state—without developing a keen antenna for the common ground and an ear for what the people wanted from their political leaders.

Another survival skill that I quickly learned as a Republican in Massachusetts is to acquire a thick skin. As my friend Andrew Natsios keeps saying, if you fall in Massachusetts politics, get up fast because the wolves will be on you in no time. I learned that if you let your critics' and opponents' charges get to you and you react in anger without thinking, you'll just give them more ammunition to fire at you. I found this to be a valuable lesson when I was being challenged and criticized by some Canadian journalists, politicians and opinion-leaders who believed that I was some sort of cowboy. I had a message to deliver on behalf of my president and the American people, and I delivered it. Public pressure works. Sometimes you just need to take your message straight to the people.

This was public diplomacy and not everyone was used to it or liked it. Many Canadians understood and appreciated the honesty. Those who didn't sometimes resorted to name-calling. But I had been called enough names during 31 years in Massachusetts politics to last a lifetime. As I told my embassy staff, this was nothing. And at all times I felt confident that most people would realize that I had paid Canadians one of the best compliments that you can pay a friend. I told them the truth, as I saw it.

Setting a New Tone

A few days after the announcement of my appointment as ambassador to Canada, a letter arrived at my office in the State House. The letter had come from John Kenneth Galbraith, one of the most remarkable men of his generation. With books like *The Affluent Society* the controversial Galbraith won world-wide prominence and immense respect as an economist and a public intellectual. He taught economics to generations of political and business leaders at Harvard; he served as the United States ambassador to India under President John F. Kennedy; and he was the author of innumerable books and articles. He continued writing even into his nineties; he had slowed down physically but his mind was sharp and his wit had not diminished one iota over the years.

The reason Galbraith wrote to me was that he is a Canadian. Born in the hamlet of Iona Station, near St. Thomas, Galbraith had left Canada as a young man but periodically returned to his native land and he had written two books about growing up in southwestern Ontario. So to some degree, he still had a foot in each country and he knew both countries and their histories. He also knew and understood the conflicts and tensions that are fundamental to Canadian–American relations, which would be the concerns of my daily life as long as I was in Canada. He had seen the news of my posting in the *Boston Globe* and invited me over to talk about Canada and about the job of being an ambassador. We spent about an hour at his home in Cambridge, near the campus of Harvard University, and in the course of our talk Galbraith gave me one piece of advice that I took to heart during my time in Canada; it was fundamental to my concept of public diplomacy, the task that would absorb me throughout my tenure in Ottawa.

"When you're the ambassador," he said, "you have to get out of the capital and see the country and meet the people." This is what he had done during his time as ambassador to India. There is a strong temptation to stay in the capital, where most other diplomats and politicians spend their time, he said. But that's not how you get to know a place and its culture. He urged me to travel as much as I could, to meet as many people as I could. I could not have had better advice. If I was going to carry out my commitment to public diplomacy, I would have to get out of Ottawa and deliver the American message across the country. That was what I was determined to do.

Canada's ambassadors are, with rare exceptions, career foreign service officers who have spent years learning the ropes of diplomatic life. Although three-quarters of United States ambassadors are also career foreign service officers, many of the high-profile important postings are political appointees. My immediate predecessor, Gordon Giffin, had been a lawyer in Georgia and an important political operative and fundraiser for President Bill Clinton. His predecessor, Jim Blanchard, had been a Democratic governor of

Michigan and friend of President Clinton for many years before his appointment to the post in Ottawa. Both the career officer and political appointee systems have their upside and downside. The argument for the political ambassador in the American system is that those ambassadors are much more likely to have a personal connection to the president and therefore be able to act as, and be perceived as, representing the views of the president himself. On the basis of my own experience, that would be my conclusion. Because I had known him for a long time, I always felt that I knew the mind of the president. Equally important, those Canadians who learned about my background were quick to discover my ties to President Bush. Whether or not they agreed with what I said, most people understood that I spoke for my president.

But there is, of course, a potential downside to the political appointment system. The disadvantage is that as a newly-confirmed ambassador who has probably spent a lifetime in partisan politics or business, you suddenly have to learn a job that may require a different skill set from the one that's worked for you all your life. Soon after my arrival in Ottawa Paul Wells, a columnist for the *National Post*, wrote that career politicians "are assumed to be incorrigible glad-handing louts who cannot handle the subtleties of the diplomat's trade." He generously added that the stereotype didn't apply to me.

I think the main reason I quickly adjusted to the diplomat's role was because of my personal style, which has always been fairly low-key and measured. But just in case there's any awkwardness, the State Department has what it hopes is a remedy. This is "ambassador school," the State Department's course for new ambassadors. So Jan and I went back to school. There were 10 others in the class along with spouses. Among the more illustrious members of my class were

Howard Baker, longtime Republican senator from Tennessee and former majority leader of the United States Senate and his wife Nancy Kassebaum, longtime Republican senator for Kansas. Howard and Nancy were headed for Japan. Margaret Tutwiler, former spokesperson for the State Department, had been nominated as United States ambassador to Morocco.

Having Jan there helped a lot, because our learning styles are very different and, fortunately for me, complementary. We all received a stack of books and documents at the beginning of the course, which suited Jan just fine. She is a voracious reader. So I was less diligent about doing the assigned readings than I should have been, but I knew that I could count on Jan to point out the most important parts. When it came to taking notes in class, Jan probably wrote 10 pages for every one of mine. Some of what we covered was interesting and useful, like our briefing from Diplomatic Security. But there were times when the subject was tedious and even silly—such as the admonition to keep an eye on dinner guests so that they don't pocket the official residence cutlery.

Jan complained that I was an ill-behaved student and that I would make a show of taking out my watch and checking the time during talks. In fact, she remembers that I actually got up and went to the washroom when one speaker was starting on an example that pertained to Canada. However, at the end of our two weeks of classes Nancy Kassebaum said to Jan that her husband would like to copy my notes. Jan's response was, "All 11 words of them?" There were more than 11 words. And they were important points.

There were a few anxious days when my nomination was before the Senate for approval. Led by Jesse Helms, a number of senators took issue with my past support of gay rights and the right to abortion. However, I was helped by the fact that mine was the new administration's first ambassadorial nomination—and helped also, I suspect, by the fact that on either side of me were the two senators from Massachusetts, both Democrats, Edward Kennedy and John Kerry. A few people, Republicans and Democrats alike, jokingly suggested that Kennedy and Kerry were just trying to get me out of Massachusetts. Who knows? But my nomination was confirmed by the Senate on April 5, 2001, and I was duly sworn in as ambassador on April 10 in the old Executive Building on the grounds of the White House. After the brief ceremony, Jan and I, Kate and Anne, and my mom and dad visited with the president in the Oval Office and the Rose Garden. Quite by accident, I proceeded to stump my new boss on a baseball trivia question. As a former owner of the Texas Rangers, the president prides himself on his baseball knowledge. Hideo Nomo of the Boston Red Sox had just thrown a no-hitter on April 4 and was pitching again that evening. I told the president that he was going for the record. The president said, "What record?" I told him that only one major leaguer had thrown back-to-back no-hitters. The president thought a bit and then suggested Ewell Blackwell, a pitcher for the Cincinnati Reds in the 1940s. "Good try," I said, "but it was Johnny Vander Meer of the Cincinnati Reds." Vander Meer had pitched no-hitters on June 11, 1938 versus the Boston Braves and June 15 versus the Brooklyn Dodgers. My dad added that he was at the game at Braves Field in Boston when Vander Meer next pitched. He said that Vander Meer went three more innings before the Braves got a hit. Maybe that wasn't a good move, stumping the boss one hour into the job, but I suspect the president was impressed that my dad and I knew our baseball.

President Bush was generous with his time that afternoon; we spent about 30 minutes talking and posing for photos in the Rose Garden. My favorite photo taken that day is of the president talking to my mom. My mother's quiet, unassuming personality was quite different from my dad's extroverted style. It was wonderful to see her talking comfortably about her family to the leader of the free world.

Jan and I arrived in Ottawa on April 16, 2001. The next day we flew to Quebec City where I presented my credentials to Governor General Adrienne Clarkson on a beautiful spring day. Three days later, I ran up the steps of Air Force One and into the cabin to greet the president on his arrival in Quebec City for the Summit of the Americas. I said, "Welcome to Canada, Mr. President." He started laughing. He knew that I had been in Canada for less than one week. A few minutes later Jan and I were sitting in Marine One, the President's helicopter, waiting to fly to the Citadel. Andy Card looked at me and said, "Don't start laughing." I knew what he meant. Two former state representatives from Massachusetts on Marine One: Andy as chief of staff to the president of the United States and me the United States ambassador to Canada. I guess we had come a long way from our days driving the president's father from campaign stop to campaign stop in 1979 and 1980.

Ottawa was now home, but it would be a while before we could move into the ambassador's residence, the 32-room limestone mansion overlooking the Ottawa and Gatineau rivers, with a spectacular view northwards to the Gatineau Hills. Originally built in 1908 by Warren Soper, owner of the Ottawa Electric Railway Company, the house sits on 12 rolling, tree-studded acres on the edge of the fashionable Rockcliffe Park. Breathtaking is not an exaggeration.

In fact I had visited the Residence in October, 1997, on a trade mission along with several Massachusetts businessmen. Although I had been to Montreal, Quebec City and Halifax on several occasions, that was my first visit to Canada's beautiful capital city. We had a buffet luncheon at the ambassador's residence, hosted by the deputy chief of mission, Mary Ann Peters. My predecessor, Gordon Giffin, was traveling at the time.

It never crossed my mind that this impressive official residence would some day be my home. I do remember, however, that despite the grandeur of the ambassador's residence it had a wonderful welcoming ambience and charm. Having lived there for four years I now realize that this is largely due to the very human scale of the rooms, the abundance of warm wood throughout the house and the postcard views from the tall windows that overlook the grounds surrounding the house. However, rather than the particular features, what I remember best from that first visit was the sheer comfort of the house.

Even though I was now ambassador, Jan and I wouldn't be able to call the official residence home for several weeks more. What we hadn't expected was the discovery of asbestos in the Residence; that prolonged our stay at the Chateau Laurier for another couple of weeks. The first time Jan saw the Rockcliffe residence there was still a large warning sign duct-taped to the front door: "*Danger! Risque de cancer et de maladie pulmonaire.*" Welcome to Ottawa.

The elegant Chateau Laurier hotel has been a commanding presence in Ottawa for generations, and anyone who has stayed there knows that it certainly isn't a hardship post. So we weren't complaining. As well as being strikingly beautiful, the Chateau's location is perfect—right in the center of Ottawa, beside Parliament Hill and just around the corner from the US Embassy and the lively Byward Market. Jan and I got to know the heart of the capital, visiting the shops along Elgin and Sparks streets, strolling along the Rideau Canal in the evening, and having a glass of wine in the market's cafés. When my best friend and barber, Bob Yesue, and his wife, Jan, visited us on the Memorial Day weekend, we were proud to show them a city that was already feeling like home. We visited the Aviation Museum, which aficionados of vintage aircraft acknowledge to be one of the best in the world, and we dined in Ottawa's "Little Italy" district. I was happy to discover that Ottawa has many notable Italian restaurants.

Getting to know the city was a pleasure. But we weren't on vacation. From the time Jan and I arrived, it was down to work, meeting my staff at the embassy, planning an itinerary of speeches and visits across Canada, and working on what would be the issues and policies that I would advocate on behalf of the president and the American people. The US embassy has the largest staff of any diplomatic mission in Ottawa, about 250 personnel. Many of these people are foreign service officers, but the staff also includes a large number of Canadians whose understanding of their country and specialized expertise are indispensable to the work of the embassy.

My transition from Massachusetts politician to US ambassador to Canada was aided immensely by the excellent team I worked with. Jan and I had already seen them in action at the Summit of the Americas in Quebec City a few days after our arrival in Canada, so we knew that this was a professional and skilled team. The United States embassy in Ottawa is a mini–US government. There are all the traditional State Department sections—political, economic and consular affairs—as well as a regional security office, including a detachment of United States marines, and information systems and administrative sections. The United States Department of Commerce and the Department of Agriculture are also there. So too is the military, represented by the United States air force, army and navy, joined recently by the US coast guard. Law enforcement is an important part of Mission Canada. The FBI, the Drug Enforcement Administration, the Department of Alcohol, Tobacco and Firearms, the Secret Service, and Customs and Immigration, now part of Homeland Security, are all part of the embassy team. Along with our seven consulates in Halifax, Quebec City, Montreal, Toronto, Winnipeg, Calgary and Vancouver and our pre-clearance facilities at seven Canadian airports, more than 1,000 people came under my chief of mission authority.

Thankfully I worked with an experienced and effective deputy chief of mission, Steve Kelly. I had met Steve during that 1997 trade mission to Canada, when my Massachusetts delegation went to Quebec City where he was the United States consul-general. The DCM is chief of staff and chief operating officer all rolled into one. Steve's strong management skills and his ability to keep me constantly advised on all aspects of our work enabled me to conduct the public diplomacy across Canada that I believed was the most important part of my job.

When Steve left in the summer of 2004, I chose John Dickson to take his place. John had been DCM in Mexico City and interestingly, in what amounted to a big league trade, Steve Kelly left to become the DCM in Mexico. John did not miss a beat. He too had strong management skills, was unflappable, and adjusted quickly to my management style. Another key person at the embassy for the ambassador is his office management specialist (OMG). Karen Heide did an excellent job managing the massive flow of mail, cables, and documents directed to me and overseeing my demanding schedule.

Not long after we arrived in Ottawa I discovered that part of the work of an ambassador involves attending and hosting social functions. That, of course, could be as much work as pleasure. My first reception was the annual California Wine Fair. It was in the main ballroom of the Chateau Laurier, a quick trip down the elevator from the suite where we were still staying. The California Wine Fair is the largest wine-tasting event in Canada, each year visiting virtually all of Canada's largest cities. There were about 500 people milling around under the elaborate chandeliers in the Chateau's richly paneled ballroom, tasting more than 180 wines from 65 California wineries. It was fun and I met some people with whom I would develop good friendships and important working relationships over the next few years. I chatted with Joe Clark, the former prime minister and then once more leader of the Progressive Conservative Party, and we clinked glasses of a full-bodied Napa red. He and his wife, Maureen McTeer, had spent several months in the San Francisco region a decade earlier and had visited many wineries in the Napa and Sonoma valleys. They had a good knowledge of West Coast wines.

Jan and I were still in the meet-and-greet phase of our time in Ottawa when we decided there had to be some kind of reception to launch us officially onto the Ottawa social scene. We had still not moved into the Residence, so Steve Kelly held a reception at his official residence for about 60 people whom I would get to know and work with over the next four years. That's the size of function I like best, where there is a real opportunity to meet and talk to everyone in the room. Among the guests were Eddie Goldenberg, Prime Minister Chrétien's right-hand man, Speaker of the House of Commons Peter Milliken, and Deputy Prime Minister Herb Gray, as well as several other members of the Liberal government. Ward Elcock, director of the Canadian Security Intelligence Service was there and also Giuliano Zaccardelli, head of the RCMP. I knew we would work closely with the RCMP and CSIS, but little did I know how important that work would be in stopping future terrorist attacks.

There were also some Ottawa scribes present. Lawrence Martin, who has covered Canada–United States affairs and who has written books on the subject, seemed to see the evening as something out of *The Great Gatsby*. "In their silent limousines," he wrote, "Ottawa's most powerful men have arrived.... They're in buoyant spirits, smug in a rug, as they welcome Paul Cellucci." He was certainly right that the mood was upbeat.

I think Martin was wrong, though, in his interpretation of why people were in such good spirits. In his newspaper column the next day he seemed to suggest that the Republican grip on power in Washington was precarious and slipping, only months after President Bush's election. Senator Jeffords of Vermont has just defected to the Democrats, producing a 50/50 partisan split in that legislative chamber, and I suppose that like a lot of Canadians Martin may have believed that my party's control of the White House was still under the cloud of the 2000 election. He may have been right in his assessment that some of those at this power reception believed that President Bush's hand would be weakened on such contentious bilateral issues as continental missile defense and energy. But that wasn't my reading of the good mood in the room. And it certainly wasn't my reading of the situation in Washington.

Our guests came from a broad political spectrum. One was Gilles Duceppe, leader of separatist Bloc Quebecois. I had been told that he was quite knowledgeable about baseball and hockey trivia. So naturally I asked him if he knew the name of the only major league pitcher to throw back to back no-hitters. He thought for a brief moment and said, "Johnny Vander Meer." As far as I was concerned, Gilles Duceppe was the most impressive leader in Canada. I had early on met with Commander Zaccardelli and Dawson Hovey, the commanding officer of "A" Division, the division in charge of our security. During my four years in Canada I was always impressed with and grateful for the work of the RCMP in providing protection for Jan and me, our embassy consulates, and all of our staff. I worked closely with "Zack" and Dawson, and we became good friends and golfing colleagues. Zack and I became the Italian Team. I was impressed with his leadership of the RCMP, and his commitment to integrated policing, where law enforcement officers at every level work together to significantly expand police coverage.

A few days later I met with a half dozen members of the national press gallery. I had invited them to the embassy on Sussex Drive, which had been opened under President Clinton not quite two years earlier. For most of them it was their first visit to the new embassy, a fortress of steel and glass that people seem to either love or hate. The architect, David Childs of Skidmore, Owings & Merrill, had worked on many major public and private projects, including the master plan and landscape design for the Great Mall and Constitution Gardens in Washington, D.C., the National Geographic Society Headquarters, and the new Arrivals Building at Dulles International Airport. The challenge for Childs was to design a building that would meet all the functional needs of the embassy—space for a staff of hundreds and state-of-the-art security—while making an impressive architectural statement. I think he succeeded.

The journalists had to pass through heavier security than they were used to on Parliament Hill, starting with a United States Marine at the metal gate to the embassy. We met in one of the conference rooms for what was simply intended to be a get-to-know-you session. Thirty years in politics had taught me that the care and feeding of the media is an important task. I knew that these were the men and women who would be telling Canadians about my government and Canada–United States relations during my tenure as ambassador. I didn't expect a free pass from anyone, but I wanted to be understood and to get a fair hearing. And on the whole I believe that I did.

To the half dozen journalists, I mentioned one aspect of the bigger picture of bilateral relations that President Bush wanted to emphasize. This was the idea of a continental security perimeter around our two countries, a concept that was already being discussed and advocated by some policy experts. I knew, and the reaction of the journalists confirmed this for me, that such talk was perceived by some Canadians as code for an attack on Canadian sovereignty. This was far from the intent, but I understood Canadian sensitivity on this matter and in the next four years I came face to face with that sensitivity on many occasions.

One of the journalists present at that meeting later described my approach as "diligent pragmatism" and felt that I would "exert a powerful calming influence on a bilateral relationship that's constantly in need of one." I took this as a compliment and as a fair assessment of the political style that I had worked on for over 30 years. I hope people will look back and judge that my influence was more calming than disturbing when the waters between our two countries were occasionally roiled.

However, it didn't take long before some Canadians were convinced that calm wasn't what my government and I had in mind. My first major policy speech was on energy, a topic that I knew was a potential minefield—although I have always believed Canada and the US have parallel interests in the energy field. As governor of Massachusetts I had been well aware of the trade in energy between our economies. In addition to importing hydro-electric power from Quebec, my home state bought lots of natural gas that was shipped south by pipeline. I knew Canada had some of the most extensive energy resources in the world and that we in the United States were Canada's best customer; I knew also that the appetite of the United States for Canadian energy was why the energy sector was as big and important as it had become in Canada. Supply and jobs don't materialize without demand, and much of that demand was coming from the United States. I knew that some Canadians had long worried about an energy grab by their southern neighbors, fearing that somehow they would lose control over this vital economic sector or, worse, that non-renewable energy resources would be gobbled up to meet the demands of American consumers. Energy was certainly going to be an area where I would be facing diplomatic challenge.

Inevitably, energy was the issue of the day when I spoke to a breakfast meeting at the National Press Club in Ottawa on June 12, 2001, just two months after my arrival in my new job. The White House had identified a more secure supply of energy as an important goal of President Bush's first term, and my press club speech was the first stage of an orchestrated effort to raise the profile of this issue with our number one energy partner. So I talked about the president's plan for a better integrated North American energy market, through more pipelines and energy infrastructure connecting Canadian sources of supply to US markets. Vice-President Cheney talked about the same plan when he met with Alberta's premier Ralph Klein at the White House two of days later. This energy initiative was centered on governments letting the markets decide what projects made sense; the role of governments then would be to issue permits as efficiently as possible to get things rolling. We knew that there was a lot of interest in this on the part of provincial governments in Canada, both in the West and the East.

The next day I was on a plane to Halifax to speak at an energy forum that Nova Scotia premier John Hamm had organized. The forum was chaired by former Alberta premier Peter Lougheed and brought together men and women from industry and government. My message was simple: You have the energy. We need it.

This was just months after the 2001 power shortage in California that had resulted in brown-outs and rolling black-outs, as well as draconian conservation measures over the winter and spring. By way of personal experience I told the energy forum about the near-crisis in my home state two years earlier. Massachusetts had come within 10 days of running out of home heating oil. If a cold snap or blizzard had hit unexpectedly we probably would have run out of oil. I went on to tell them that gas from Sable Island had had a very stabilizing effect on energy supply and prices in Massachusetts during my last winter as governor. Many large commercial users had been able to shift from heating oil to gas, so the danger of running out of fuel wasn't hanging over our heads. This also meant that we didn't experience the spike in energy prices that had sent us reeling two winters earlier. So I knew first hand the importance of Canadian energy supplies. I think that probably enhanced my credibility as the messenger for the president's energy plan.

This was the first of several speeches that I gave during my early months as ambassador, when I talked to Canadians and their leaders about the bigger picture of economic integration or what I called NAFTA-plus. The connecting theme in all of these speeches was that Canada, the United States and Mexico should build on the successes of the free trade agreement for the mutual benefit of the people of all three countries. In the case of energy, we were clear about what we had in mind. Our goal was to enable markets to work better, and not to create a continental energy policy that would threaten Canadian sovereignty. Of course, that didn't stop some critics from misrepresenting our intentions. But the White House was categorical in stating that the choice of pipeline route and other major infrastructure decisions in Canada should be made in Canada and in response to market forces.

In addition to my energy speeches I addressed the Council of Great Lakes Governors. This type of meeting is near and dear to me. As governor of Massachusetts I always looked forward to the annual meeting of the New England governors and Eastern Canadian premiers, getting to know them and their issues well. So even before coming to Canada I had a comfortable working relationship with Canadian premiers and felt an affinity with them and the sorts of challenges they faced. I find that there is more partisanship and ideological locking of horns in national politics, in both Canada and in the United States, than at the regional level. Provincial and state governments are more results-focused. Some of this difference may be due to the different issues that are dealt with at the regional and national levels. But I think a large part of it is due to the national media spotlight that is always shining on federal politicians in both countries. That spotlight is more likely to create intransigence than a willingness to compromise, as political leaders respond to constant demands of the press.

The day after she arrived in Ottawa Jan attended the annual meeting of the Association of Research Librarians in Toronto. She saw our time in Canada as an opportunity to make a contribution to Canada's system of research libraries, visiting library directors and examining library collections and services across the country, and discussing efforts to persuade Canadian decision-makers to recognize the importance of libraries. When we traveled to Canadian cities where I would be giving a speech, Jan took the opportunity to visit the university library there and meet with fellow librarians. (I came to notice that these visits often seemed to be timed so that Jan had to miss my speech. Pure coincidence, I suppose.)

A daunting task after our arrival in Ottawa was planning the annual Fourth of July celebration at the official residence. Under my predecessor, Gordon Giffin, this had become a huge affair. The crowd at the previous year's celebration was estimated at more than 5,000.

In planning our party we wanted to limit the size of the guest list so that we could actually meet all our guests. We invited about 1,500 politicians, diplomats, US citizens and friends. We decided on a New England flavor for the event: cod cakes, Yankee pot roast soup, lobster ravioli, maple-roasted pork loin from Vermont, cherrystone clams, lobster, clam chowder and, of course, Boston Cream pie. We offered California wines but there was also Samuel Adams beer. Jan was so busy hosting that she didn't find time to eat a bite. But I tasted just about everything, so I was able to tell her what delicious food she missed. By the end of the evening we looked around the crowd and realized that with the invaluable help of our embassy and residence staff we had indeed managed to meet everyone there. Among our guests were our two daughters, Anne and Kate, along with Anne's roommate at Harvard, Talhia Tuck. Talhia sang the American and Canadian national anthems, and she did it beautifully. I departed from the tradition of reading the president's Independence Day speech and instead made spontaneous remarks about the similarities of our two great countries and our mutual commitment to freedom and democracy. I ended my brief speech with "Vive le Canada. Vive the United States."

With Parliament recessed for the summer and the arrival of sunny, hot days, the rhythm of life in Ottawa seems to shift gears as the tourists take over the cafés, the canal and Parliament Hill. But at the embassy we had a lot of work to do. The United States has seven consulates across Canada and I wanted to visit all of them as soon as possible. These visits would provide me with opportunities to do public diplomacy.

So during what would generally be the slow news months of the summer I was traveling to our consulates in Montreal, Vancouver, Calgary, Toronto and Halifax giving policy speeches in each of these cities. If my audiences expected fluffy speeches with little more than diplomatic niceties they were in for a surprise. These were serious explorations of Canada–United States relations and the directions that my government hoped to see those relations take.

I started to sketch this bigger picture by the end of June 2001. I was explaining and defending the president's National Energy Policy Report. This report was about a lot more than future energy supply. It is a blueprint for addressing serious constraints on economic growth for the next two decades, and preventing US and Canadian citizens' quality of life from being disrupted by poor policies, outdated infrastructure, and environmental degradation. Wherever I went I quoted Jeffrey Rubin, the chief economist of CIBC World Markets, as saying that "no one will benefit more from this brave new direction in US energy policy than Canada." That was the message that I wanted to get across to our Canadian friends.

I also repeated my government's belief that Canada, the United States and Mexico should be looking at ways to deepen the economic integration between them through a NAFTA-plus relationship based on better harmonization of border controls, law enforcement and energy, environmental and immigration policies.

I was not alone in suggesting such changes. Ideas like those were increasingly in the air. David Zussman, president of the Public Policy Forum and a policy adviser to Prime Minister Chrétien, had already called for a public debate on economic and social union between Canada, the United States and Mexico. "Canadians in all parts of civil society should actively encourage a growing debate over new ideas, which, until a few years ago, were completely taboo in respectable Canadian society," Zussman said in a speech he gave in Calgary. Anthony DePalma, who spent several years in Canada as a correspondent for the *New York Times*, had just published a book called *Here: A Biography of the New North American Continent*. In it he made a compelling case for the inevitability and desirability of continued economic integration.

But when the United States ambassador starts to preach such ideas, some Canadians become suspicious. "US hopes to erase borders" was one of the headlines. "US presses for stronger ties," read another. The *Montreal Gazette* came closest to getting it right: "US ambassador rejects union, but calls for harmony in Canada, US border policies." I made clear my belief that the kind of harmonization I was talking about would not lead to a formal political union between Canada and the United States or even an open-border, common-currency model as in the European Union.

Of course that didn't stop some people from assuming hidden agendas. Lorne Nystrom, longtime NDP member of Parliament from Saskatchewan, was quoted as saying, "I'm beginning to suspect that there is an orchestrated move to soften us up toward political and economic integration with the US." The nationalist Council of Canadians reacted with full-blown paranoia, calling the United States "the biggest bully in town and in the world" and warning that greater economic integration and policy harmonization between our two countries would lead to Canada becoming completely dominated by the United States.

So just as millions of Canadians were getting ready to head out on vacation I was making headlines by simply advocating more open and creative thinking on the future of the Canada–United States relationship. The idea of NAFTA-plus would be the centerpiece of what I planned to communicate to Canadians over the months to come. I had already talked to Transport Minister David Collenette about my government's interest in expanding the existing "open skies" agreement on flights between our two countries. And I intended to keep making speeches about the bigger picture of a North American perimeter, as well as specific measures to advance this goal.

In addition to promoting the economic advantages of NAFTA-plus, I wanted to quell the fears of some Canadians that this would lead to the obliteration of Canada's distinctive culture and institutions. So in August I made the point that one of the paradoxes of economic integration is that it tends to increase the importance of social, cultural and political differences between nations. I said that globalization did not appear to have made Serbs less Serb or Spaniards less Spanish. If anything, greater economic integration appeared to make national populations more appreciative of their own cultures, while increased communication and travel between nations broadens the awareness and understanding of other cultures. The claim that economic integration would necessarily lead to some sort of leveling of cultural differences was not, I argued, supported by either logic or the facts.

I was pleased that these ideas were getting a hearing in the Canadian press. George Haynal, the Canadian co-chair of the Canada–United States Partnership, an advisory group that reports directly to the prime minister and the president, gave my public diplomacy initiative a boost by supporting the continental perimeter concept. "We should push it as far as we can," he told the *National Post*. William Watson, McGill University professor and one of Canada's most respected economists, helped keep the momentum going with a long newspaper piece on NAFTA-plus. "Border debate picking up speed: MPs nearest US favour integration," was the headline of one newspaper article. The article went on to note that support for the idea of greater integration could be found in all parties, except the NDP. I agreed wholeheartedly with the sentiments of Conservative MP Rick Borostik, who was quoted as saying "I don't think a border crossing is what makes us Canadian. If you look at the European model, Germany is still Germany.... They can certainly maintain a cultural identity without anybody saying, 'Are you going for business or pleasure?'"

By the end of that first summer, less than six months into the job, I was encouraged with the debate that was taking place on NAFTA-plus. My goal was to generate more open thinking on ways to reduce economic barriers between our two countries, to reduce the cost of doing business and to improve the quality of life for both Canadians and Americans. Measured against that goal, my public diplomacy seemed to be off to a good start.

Another side of my public diplomacy campaign that summer was my call for a much bolder and clearer defence policy. For decades successive governments had been easing the pressure on their tax dollars by cutting defence spending; those cuts were accelerated by the end of the Cold War and growing budgetary deficits. The political convenience of cutting defence spending was obvious, but these cutbacks had reached the point where Canada's military forces were in danger of losing much of their effectiveness.

My warnings on defense were delivered with confidence. The only specific instruction Secretary of State Colin Powell had given me before I came to Canada was about defense spending. The former chief of the United States Armed Forces told me that Canada's forces were very capable in combat operations and peacekeeping assignments, but that reduced spending was taking a toll on their effectiveness. He told me bluntly to try to get the Canadian government to spend much more on defence, and that was what I tried to do on virtually every platform to which I was invited. It was a long and difficult campaign.

I was not the first American official to make such observations. My predecessor, Gordon Giffin, had made similar remarks during his tenure in Ottawa. But, for various reasons, my comments touched off a firestorm in Canada, one that would wax and wane over the remainder of my time as ambassador. Diplomatic fire and brimstone seemed to be what was expected of me. The *Ottawa Sun* described my remarks as a "rhetorical cruise missile." I was pleased, however, that most Canadian media seemed to welcome my suggestion that Canada had to reinvest in its military if it wanted to maintain its credibility and influence abroad. David Pratt, Liberal chair of the Commons defence committee, reacted by saying, "What Mr. Cellucci has said is basically some of the things we [on the committee] have been saying." He went on to say what many Canadians might not have wanted to hear, but which I was glad they heard from him rather than me or another American spokesperson: "If we don't spend more money on defence we risk a loss of sovereignty to the US."

Five months into my job as ambassador I was comfortable with the way things were going. The emphasis on public diplomacy suited my style. I enjoyed delivering a message on behalf of my president and the American people. And the results were positive. Some of the broad themes that we wanted to get onto the table were being aired and were even receiving a favorable reaction from Canadians and their opinion leaders.

Then came September 11, 2001, and the message became more urgent.

CHAPTER FOUR

Shoulder to Shoulder

When terrorists struck at the heart of America on September 11, 2001, there was a valuable lesson—perhaps many valuable lessons—to be learned about the relationship between the United States and Canada. The immediate lesson was that the instinct of Canadians was to help their neighbors in whatever way they could. Most of the world felt horror and revulsion at the death of almost 3,000 innocent people who died because they went to work that day, but Canadians may have felt it more acutely simply because they are neighbors and the bonds between the two countries are too numerous to count. So Prime Minister Chrétien called as soon as he heard about the attacks, offering whatever help was needed. When hundreds of American flights were diverted to Canada because American air space had been closed to all air traffic, 25,000 American passengers suddenly found themselves stranded in Canada, sometimes in fairly remote communities; hundreds of Canadians simply turned up at their local airports to offer food and shelter to the stranded Americans. The spontaneous outpouring of sympathy, generosity and goodwill from friends and even total strangers was overwhelming. For Jan and me and everyone at the embassy, seeing the Maple Leaf flying at half-mast all over Ottawa in solidarity with the Stars and Stripes touched us in ways difficult to express. That reminder of friendship will remain as one of my most treasured memories of our time in Ottawa.

But there were other lessons to be learned — or, more correctly, old lessons to be remembered. Above all, Canada is affected by almost every major change within the United States; in some way, any change stateside may bring unintended consequences for the northern neighbor. Former Prime Minister Pierre Trudeau put it best long ago when he said that living beside the United States is like sleeping beside an elephant. This is not to suggest hostility but sensitivity; Canada is ever watchful for those unintended consequences, for any grunt or groan that might suggest that the elephant is about to roll over. Certainly an American ambassador in Ottawa must be constantly aware of those sensitivities — and I thought I was aware — but I admit that I was surprised by how quickly the suspicions of some Canadians were aroused in the aftermath of September 11.

For both the US and Canada, the events of September 11 were a wake-up call. For the five months that I had been in Ottawa, I had been talking about a common security perimeter, smart border technology, and more common policies on immigration and refugee standards. Suddenly there was about all those concerns a new and terrible urgency. The lines of trucks at the Windsor–Detroit border crossing, which stretched for miles in the days after the attacks, were a stark reminder of how long the world's greatest trading relationship had simply been taken for granted. But, looking back, what is striking is how well the authorities on both sides of the border reacted to the situation and how quickly and effectively they moved to make sure that goods and people could continue to move between our two countries. Fear and paralysis are what terrorists are seeking. When the president spoke to Americans and the world on the morning of September 12, he delivered a message of reassurance: those who tried to cripple the spirit of Americans through their heinous acts would not succeed.

That afternoon I met the press corps in Ottawa. The press office at the embassy had been inundated with requests for interviews and comments. We decided that a press conference would be the best solution. As I entered the room and took my seat between the flags of Canada and the United States, there was none of the usual murmur of conversation among the journalists. The mood was somber and uncertain. Unfounded rumors that the terrorists might have entered the United States from Canada were already circulating and there were many more questions than answers about the days ahead. I began by thanking the Canadian government and the Canadian people for their immediate cooperation and support. This was the first of many occasions that I would have over the next three years to express the gratitude of my government and the American people for the remarkable generosity and aid that Canada had shown in our hour of need.

The questions asked that day reflected a sense that we as citizens of free and open societies had been pushed across a new threshold. Canadians and Americans were frightened and angry. They were used to feeling safe when boarding a commercial airline. They were used to feeling secure when they went to work in a high-rise office building. We had to make sure, I said, that the citizens of both of our countries and the citizens of countries around the globe could continue to feel safe when they do such everyday things.

The questions at the press conference moved quickly into that broad area of particular Canadian sensitivity—the possible repercussions of the terrorist attacks on Canada–United States relations. What would be the impact of the attacks on the NAFTA-plus initiative that I had been promoting over the previous months? Would there be reprisals for Canada, such as tighter border restrictions, if it was discovered that some of those who hijacked the planes or participated in planning the attacks had entered the United States from Canada? The case of Ahmed Ressam, the Algerian terrorist who had tried to enter the United States at the border crossing between British Columbia and Washington with a trunk full of explosives on a mission to blow up Los Angeles Airport, was specifically mentioned by some journalists. And the sensitive issue of differences in Canadian and American immigration policies was also raised.

The thrust of my message that day was straightforward. I said it was the policy of the United States government to make sure that law-abiding citizens and commerce could continue to move freely between our two countries. At the same time, the attacks on the World Trade Center and the Pentagon underlined the urgency of pressing ahead on the policy reforms that I had been advocating over the previous five months. We needed to move toward more common immigration policies, better intelligence sharing and law enforcement, and working together on a number of fronts to better protect the people and prosperity of our countries. This did not mean that Canada and the United States would have to agree on everything. Prime Minister Chrétien had said the day before, when asked about the need for a common immigration policy, that "US officials are in charge of people entering the United States and Canadian officials are in charge of people entering Canada." I agreed. I had been saying for months that a more common immigration policy did not mean the elimination of all differences or the sacrifice of either country's sovereignty. But in the shadow of September 11 it had become hard to argue against taking a hard look at ways to prevent the entry of those who wanted to enter Canada or the United States for illegal purposes.

Canadians and Americans wanted reassurance that their leaders would take effective steps to deal with terrorism, but they also needed to grieve. Prime Minister Chrétien declared September 14 a national day of mourning for the victims of the terrorist attacks. The scene that day was unforgettable. There was not even a hint of suspicion or uneasiness about relations between the two countries. The mournful silence of the thousands on Parliament Hill was powerful beyond words. Only the sound of the carillon bells from the Peace Tower broke the stillness.

Prime Minister Chrétien spoke first. "We will be with the United States every step of the way," he said. "As friends. As neighbors. As family." After the prime minister it was my turn to address the thousands of Canadians and Americans who stood shoulder to shoulder that day. Sadness, incredulity, defiance and perseverance marked the faces in the crowd. Clearly, the people who stood silently on Parliament Hill had grown older in the last days. It was the most emotional occasion on which I ever had to speak. I believe my words that day expressed the sorrow, but also the hope and defiance that we all felt in the face of the evil that had taken the lives of so many innocent people.

As a Scottish piper played a mournful tune I could see the emotion on the faces of the thousands of men and women around us. Governor General Clarkson called for three minutes of silence to honor the victims of the attacks. I don't think anyone could have believed that a crowd so large could be so profoundly quiet. It was the deep tolling of the Peace Tower bells that finally broke the silence and ended the ceremony.

That evening, Jan and I invited the embassy family to the official residence for a prayer service. We were both feeling the absence of our daughters and extended family during such a trying and emotional time. Having the house filled with colleagues and their children, eating cookies, drinking soda and coffee and just being together, was a comfort for both of us.

That was a day for grieving, but even on such an emotional day questions of policy arose. That afternoon a journalist had asked me about the charge from Stockwell Day, leader of the Opposition, that the Canadian government appeared unwilling to give an unequivocal commitment of military support to the US government. My reply was clear: "I don't think you can get more unequivocal than [the prime minister's] statement today—side by side, every step of the way." Chrétien's statement was very strong and on behalf of my government and the American people I was very grateful. In the months that followed, the Prime Minister was as good as his word. Canada was an important member of the NATO coalition that routed the Taliban from Afghanistan and restored freedom to a country whose people had been under the heel of repression and which had become a haven and training ground for al Qaeda terrorists. When the news of the terrorist attacks reached the prime minister the morning of September 11, his words were, "The world just changed." These were the words of a national leader who appreciated the enormity of what had happened and knew what had to be done.

I knew, however, that Prime Minister Chrétien would have to fend off fears that cooperation with the US on such matters as immigration and border security would require a surrender of Canadian sovereignty. I didn't see how action to protect the security and prosperity of Canadians could reasonably be interpreted as a sacrifice of national sovereignty, but I was familiar enough with the political terrain to know that this was an issue the Canadian government would have to face, and American diplomats should tread with caution.

A lot of the debate in those first days and weeks focused on the issue of immigration policy. In Canada's House of Commons and in the media, the debate brought out the full spectrum of the politics of Canada–United States relations. At one end were people like Liberal MP Maurizio Bevilacqua, then chair of the House Finance Committee, who warned that Canadians might have to "step outside their comfort zones" to elevate the level of national, continental and global security. At the other end were people like NDP leader Alexa McDonough. At a rally in Toronto a week after the terrorist attacks, McDonough told a crowd of university students that the United States did not have the moral authority to pursue terrorists and that Canadian policies should be unchanged.

My position and that of the Bush government was straightforward. We wanted to see more consistent immigration and refugee policies between our two countries. We would each make sovereign decisions on immigration — how many immigrants, from which countries, with what skills — but we would put in place common security standards so that we knew who we were welcoming. Such common security standards were something that I had been advocating even before September 11, but the terrorist attacks made this more urgent. I reminded Canadians that security is a two-way street, but that the street sometimes has odd twists and turns. For example, Canada required visas for visitors from some countries where the United States did not, and vice versa. I took the position that fighting terrorism and crime was in both countries' interests. Our policies would not have to be exactly the same, but a more common approach would mean that we could maintain an open border. With more than $1.5 billion in trade moving between our countries each day, I believed reasonable people understood what was at stake.

It was not long before the media on both sides of the border started using the term "Fortress America" and "Fortress North America." The *Toronto Star* accused me of pushing such a proposal, but that was not at all what I had been urging. The common security perimeter that I had been advocating since my arrival in Ottawa was never about walling off North America from the rest of the world. Instead, the purpose was to better identify and screen out the tiny fraction of those entering our countries who come with the intent to do us harm or break the law. This seemed the best way to preserve our open societies and the free flow of people and trade across our common border. Few Canadians, I believe, would argue with that.

I know that fears about loss of sovereignty are deeply embedded in the Canadian psyche; such fears are not likely to be swept away by arguments about the war on terrorism. So I knew that Prime Minister Chrétien would have to walk a tightrope at home to satisfy Canadians' desire for greater security without giving up their independence. In reply to a question in the House of Commons about the need for greater harmonization of Canadian and American immigration policies, the prime minister offered, "There is one thing I want to say. The laws of Canada will be passed by the Parliament of Canada." This was, I thought, a fair and pragmatic position that reflected the balance of values that Canadians wanted to see expressed in their national policies. An Ekos poll taken after September 11 found that 53 percent of Canadians favored the creation of a Canada–US security perimeter "even if it means we must effectively accept American security and immigration policies." I knew that this level of support was probably inflated by the fresh shock and anger unleashed by the terrorist attacks. But I also believed that Canadian public opinion had been genuinely moved by the attacks and by the realities of the war on terror. Polls showed that the vast majority of Canadians believed that their lives would be "deeply and permanently changed by these terrorist attacks" and public support was extremely high for measures to coordinate immigration policy, including common entry controls for visitors to our two countries, harmonization of visa requirements, and photo-ID cards for landed immigrants in Canada.

The day after Prime Minister Chrétien's statement during Question Period, President Bush addressed Congress in a televised speech. The President specifically thanked a number of countries that had agreed to help the United States in this new war against terrorism. Many countries were mentioned, but Canada was not among them. Listening to the speech in Ottawa, I knew that Canadian sensitivities would be sparked by such an oversight, whatever the explanation. Sure enough, the failure to mention Canada triggered a wave of indignation; many Canadians believed that Canada had been deliberately snubbed by President Bush.

In fact, there was no deliberate snub. Yes, Canada should have been mentioned. But the president's failure to do so was testimony of the unique relationship between our two countries—perhaps too easily taken for granted—rather than any kind of intended slight. President Bush was attempting to show the breadth of support for the coalition that he was building in the war against terrorism, which was why he thought it important to mention countries such as Egypt, Pakistan, India and El Salvador. Canada was considered to be like family: you know that you can always count on family when you need them. Prime Minister Chrétien knew that; he was the first world leader thanked by President Bush in a telephone call on September 12.

This was truly a tempest in a teapot. But for years afterwards I heard about what some still believed was the president's snub of Canada and his failure to acknowledge that Canada was the first to come to the aid of the United States when hundreds of flights and 25,000 American passengers were diverted to Canadian airports in the hours after the terrorist attacks. The issue should have been put to rest when Prime Minister Chrétien visited the White House two weeks after the attacks. I personally briefed the president about the effect of his failure to mention Canada in his speech; it was Chrétien who somehow inherited the crisis on that one. The president did his best. Standing shoulder to shoulder with the prime minister in front of the press, he tried to set the record straight:

> An amazing thing came up the other day. Somebody said to me, well, you know, in your speech to Congress, there were some that took affront in Canada because I didn't mention the name. I didn't think it was important to praise a brother; after all, we're talking about family.
>
> There should be no doubt in anybody's mind about how honored we are to have the support of the Canadians, and how strong the Canadian prime minister has been.
>
> And not only his condolences, but his offer of support for the American people. I guess there's somebody playing politics with you Mr. Prime Minister. But I suggest those who try to play politics with my words and drive wedges between Canada and me, understand that at this time, when nations are under attack, now is not the time for politics. Now is the time to develop a strategy to fight and win the war. And Mr. Prime Minister, I want to thank you for being here to continue those efforts with me.

During that visit I was struck by the calm, methodical, and respectful manner permeating the White House during this time of international crisis. Even as the rubble of the World Trade Center was still burning, President Bush was telling the American people that they should continue to go about their lives as usual, going to work and school, shopping, traveling and maintaining the rest of their daily routines. Disruption was what the terrorists wanted, so it was important to re-establish normalcy in people's lives. In Ottawa, I took this message to heart. Although virtually all of my official business now focused on the immediate concerns of border security, intelligence sharing and military preparedness, I knew that it would send the wrong signal if the ambassador of the United States seemed to drop out of sight and did not fulfill his social engagements. So only nine days after September 11 I attended the annual fundraising gala of the National Arts Centre. World-renowned cellist Yo-Yo Ma was the headliner. Mitchell Sharp, Liberal cabinet minister under both Lester Pearson and Pierre Trudeau, took a turn with the maestro's baton during the orchestra's encore of the overture from Mozart's *Marriage of Figaro*. My embassy supplied the Robert Mondavi wines at the evening's gourmet dinner. There had been suggestions that the event be canceled, but I believed that the NAC was doing the right thing in going forward with the event as planned. As sad as we all felt, we also knew that defiance was the proper response to those who sought to achieve their goals by spreading fear.

A week after visiting the White House, Prime Minister Chrétien and I traveled together to New York City to witness first hand the destruction at Ground Zero. The prime minister was joined by opposition party leaders Joe Clark, Stockwell Day, Gilles Duceppe and Alexa McDonough. There had been mutterings in the Canadian media about the prime minister not going to New York sooner. There were even absurd claims that this was because he and President Bush didn't get along or because of a lack of sympathy for the tragedy America had suffered. Of course, neither claim was remotely true.

The prime minister was clearly shaken by what he saw, as were we all. "It's something unbelievable," he said as he took in the horrific scene. The acrid smell of burned wire and melted plastic and death hung in the air. Jagged splinters of steel, crooked beams, crazily twisted pipes and enormous piles of rubble marked the spot where almost 3,000 people lost their lives. Cranes and bulldozers eerily moved around the site, and there were rescue workers locating and identifying bodies. Mayor Giuliani, an old friend and colleague, met us after we had toured the devastation where the twin towers had stood. "The Canadian people are with you," Prime Minister Chrétien told him. "Canadians should keep traveling. They should keep coming to New York." I remember Mayor Giuliani telling us that one of the miracles of 9/11 was that 25,000 people escaped the towers before they collapsed. Thank God for the firefighters and police officers who ran into the buildings as everyone was running out to help people escape. We continue to mourn the firefighters and police officers who lost their lives in such courageous circumstances.

After my trip with the prime minister to Ground Zero, I met with the editorial board of the *Globe and Mail*. Everyone expected that an attack on Afghanistan, where al Qaeda's terrorist training camps enjoyed the protection of the repressive Taliban regime, was imminent. What Canada's role would be in the US-led military campaign was on everyone's mind. I had already raised the problem of Canada's defense spending in a speech that I gave in August at Whistler, British Columbia, and the war on terrorism obviously injected new urgency into the issue. Canada had a proud record of participating in peacekeeping missions. However, as Canadian defense experts knew, it was a record that was becoming less tenable as a result of years of cuts to the military budget. New spending was absolutely necessary if Canada hoped to preserve its well-deserved international reputation as a peacekeeper. Yet it was also clear that even with its depleted forces Canada could play a significant combat role in any military campaign in Afghanistan.

I told the *Globe and Mail*'s editors that my government believed Canada could make a strong contribution to the war on terrorism in two important ways. One was by expanding its peacekeeping capacity, and that would certainly require more spending. It was clear that the United States would not be in a position to do as much peacekeeping as we had been doing in the past. We had over 12,000 soldiers on peacekeeping duty in Bosnia, Kosovo and Macedonia. Canada had 2,400 troops on UN and NATO peacekeeping missions, most of them in Bosnia. If, as seemed inevitable, my government shifted troops and resources to the fight against terrorism, then we would be looking to countries like Canada to do more on the peacekeeping front. I know some Canadians probably thought it was presumptuous of me to appear to lecture them on peacekeeping. But what they did not know—and what the Canadian government did not boast about—was that Canada had fallen to thirty-fifth place in the world in the number of troops it had committed to peacekeeping missions. It was important that Canada maintain and expand its combat capacity as well. The contribution of Canadian forces in a combat role in Afghanistan was significant and they performed admirably. Eight hundred and fifty soldiers forming the Third Princess Patricia's Canadian Light Infantry Battle Group fought in Operation Enduring Freedom with the Third Brigade, 187th Infantry Regiment of the US 101st Airborne Division. An additional 250 personnel, primarily Canadian air force flying supplies into Afghanistan on CC-130 Hercules aircraft, also served.

The second contribution that my government believed Canada

could make was as a diplomatic pipeline to countries whose relations with the United States were hostile. "Canada is in a lot of countries where the United States does not have a presence," I said, adding that Canada's relations with countries in the Middle East were in some cases better than ours. "It's good to know that the president can call the prime minister to say, 'Can you help me here or there?'" I had already spoken publicly about Canada performing this role, when Canada re-established formal diplomatic ties with Libya earlier that summer.

I also made the point that my government had no complaints about Canada's position on military support for the United States after the September 11 attacks. Whenever we asked for something the Canadian government responded. My comments on Canada's military forces and the direction my government wanted Canada's defense policy to take were not criticisms. They were part of the public diplomacy campaign that I had been engaged in for months. It was straight talk between friends, and talk that I believed Canadians needed to hear more of, and not just from me.

Days after my advocacy of more defense spending by Canada made headlines, Foreign Affairs Minister John Manley weighed in with his own comments on the issue. "Canada," he said, "is still trading on a reputation that was built two generations and more ago—but that we haven't continued to live up to." Speaking to the *National Post*'s Paul Wells, Manley argued that the Canadian government's intelligence-gathering, defense and foreign aid capacities were all, in his words, glaringly inadequate. "You can't just sit at the G–8 table," he said, "and then when the bill comes, go to the washroom." Influence on the world stage carries a price tag, and it was a price, Manley argued, that successive federal governments had been unwilling to pay.

Anyone who has spent a long time in politics knows that it often takes a crisis before people can be persuaded to face hard truths and take steps that may be long overdue. I think most Canadians and their leaders realized that the crisis had come and that it was time to take the steps that had been put off because a sense of urgency wasn't there. My pushing of a security perimeter, more common immigration standards, and a renewed commitment by Canada to its military forces ruffled some feathers. But there was a lot of support on Main Street, Canada for the message that I was delivering. You only had to read the letters to the editor pages of newspapers, look at the public opinion polls, and talk to Canadians in the street to know that the vast majority of them agreed with my message. Haroon Siddiqui, a columnist for the *Toronto Star* who had often been quite critical of my government and its policies, captured the mood of his compatriots: "There is an extraordinary sympathy, empathy, and walking shoulder to shoulder with the Americans."

On October 2, 2001, the 19 members of NATO met in Brussels to consider evidence compiled by the intelligence services of the United States and Great Britain concerning those responsible for the terrorist attacks of September 11. The evidence pointed overwhelmingly to Osama bin Laden and his al Qaeda network, whose patron state was Afghanistan under the Taliban. "The facts are clear and compelling," said Lord Robertson, NATO's secretary-general. "The information points conclusively to an al Qaeda role in the 11 September attacks." Canada and the other members of NATO voted unanimously to invoke Article 5 of the alliance's charter for the first time in NATO's 52-year history. This article declares that an attack on one member of NATO is an attack on all.

The same day my senior officials and I gave a classified briefing at our embassy to top-level officials from Foreign Affairs, Defence, the RCMP, the Canadian Security Intelligence Service, the Solicitor-General and the Privy Council Office. President Bush made a personal phone call to Prime Minister Chrétien, explaining the evidence linking bin Laden to the attacks. But even before this call, the prime minister had concluded that the evidence pointed to al Qaeda, based on the daily intelligence briefings that he had been receiving and earlier discussions with the president and National Security Advisor Condoleezza Rice. At a press conference in Washington, DC, Attorney General John Ashcroft, joined by Canadian Solicitor-General Lawrence MacAulay, expressed the shared resolve of our two governments. "We believe," he said, "that the roots of this act of terrorism, this act of war, are to be found in Afghanistan." Shoulder to shoulder, there was no light to be seen between our positions.

On the afternoon of October 7, President Bush addressed Americans and people throughout the world with a stern message:

> On my orders, the United States military has begun strikes against al Qaeda terrorist training camps and military installations of the Taliban regime in Afghanistan. These carefully targeted actions are designed to disrupt the use of Afghanistan as a terrorist base of operations, and to attack the military capability of the Taliban regime.
>
> We are joined in this operation by our staunch friend, Great Britain. Other close friends, including Canada, Australia, Germany and France, have pledged forces as the operation unfolds.... We are supported by the collective will of the world....
>
> The battle is now joined on many fronts. We will not waver; we will not tire; we will not falter; and we will not fail. Peace and freedom will prevail.

I knew that we could count on the support of Canadians and their government, and the president knew this too. In this war against terrorism our countries stood shoulder to shoulder.

CHAPTER FIVE

The Smart Border and Beyond

The border between the United States and Canada is one of the wonders of the political world. More than 5,000 miles, across mountains, woods, lakes, pastures, swamps, villages, even through houses—and all of it virtually undefended. As time went by, the wonders of the border seemed to become even more amazing: every year, 200 million people cross the border between the two countries, every day $1.5 billion worth of goods are shipped from one country to the other. Few questions are asked. Not much more than, Where are you going? How long will you be? Fine. Have a safe trip. The US Border Patrol had more than 9,000 agents patrolling the border between the United States and Mexico, but there were a mere 300 on duty on the US–Canada border, which is twice as long.

However, those easy days—undefended with few questions asked—were already starting to fade. And on September 11, 2001, those days ended abruptly and completely. Aside from Ground Zero in New York and the Pentagon in Washington, the evidence of the terrorist attacks was most obvious at the major Canada–US border crossing points. Papers and cargoes were suddenly being scrutinized suspiciously, and the lineups of trucks and cars stretched for miles on both sides of the border. The just-in-time delivery systems that transport parts from plants to trucks to assembly lines were paralyzed by long delays. Costs soared; factories closed and laid off their workers. Commuter traffic across the border had previously become so common that people rarely thought about the border; suddenly, from one day to the next, the 30,000 cross-border commuters were stalled. In a place like Windsor, across the river from Detroit, many people had to wake up at 4:00 a.m. to get to work on time. Nurses from Windsor who worked in Detroit began going to work in special buses that had pre-clearance at the border. It did not take much imagination to figure out that a terrorist attack at a major border crossing would have turned a difficult situation into a disaster.

Looking back over the days after September 11, what strikes me is how quickly our governments moved on border security. Although the differences between the two governments often received more media attention, the reality was that we made enormous and rapid strides to make border crossing faster and more secure. Indeed, apart from persuading the Canadian government to invest more in its military, I think of the Smart Border agreement between Canada and the United States as the most important accomplishment of my four years in Ottawa.

The explanation is not hard to find. Quite simply, inaction was no longer an option. The Canadian Security and Intelligence Service acknowledged that every known terrorist organization in the world had a Canadian branch or cell, and Canada's liberal asylum policies were a source of great concern in the US. Then there was the case of Abu Mezer, a Palestinian refugee who was caught three times sneaking into the United States from Canada before he was finally arrested in 1997 for planning to bomb the New York subway. More shocking for the US was Ahmed Ressam, who had obtained a fraudulent Canadian passport and was arrested in 1999 as he was crossing the border from Canada, on his way to blow up Los Angeles Airport. Not surprisingly there were rumors—some of them reported in the US media—that the September 11 hijackers had entered the United States from Canada; it turned out that the rumors were all false, but they increased the pressure on both governments to tighten security dramatically. Both countries would have to improve the screening of immigrants from overseas. I warned again and again that the situation was urgent and could not continue. If the border became an impediment our economic prosperity, that would just be one more way for the terrorists to win.

My own goal was to establish a more coordinated approach to border security. I got the chance to argue the case when I was invited to brief the immigration subcommittee of the United States Senate, chaired by my home state's senior senator, Ted Kennedy, in the month after the terrorist attacks. Appearing before the committee at the same time was the United States ambassador to Mexico, Jeffrey Davidow. Clearly, in the minds of the policy-makers in Washington the land borders of the United States were a real problem. My presentation to the committee was that we needed to make the land borders both more secure and at the same time more open, and we needed to create a security perimeter, a zone of confidence, around North America. As I repeatedly told audiences in Canada, "The border has to be closed to terrorists, smugglers and drug pushers, but it has to be open for trade, for tourism and for legitimate family travel."

Later in the day I met with Director of Homeland Security Tom Ridge at the White House. Tom and I knew each other since our time as governors and we had both worked on the president's 2000 campaign. He was the first enlisted Vietnam combat veteran elected to the US House of Representatives. Like me, Tom was a tax cutter and a leader who, during his time as governor, emphasized standards and accountability in public education. After September 11, the president asked Tom to become the first director of homeland security and then the first cabinet secretary of homeland security in 2002. We are both serious football fans, although we haven't always found ourselves rooting for the same team, as when the New England Patriots met the Philadelphia Eagles in the 2005 Super Bowl. But this was a day for discussing the urgency of better border security.

A window of opportunity had opened as a result of the tragedy of 9/11. I saw my job as championing the idea of a zone of confidence between our countries. This was the message that I took to Senator Kennedy and the members of the immigration subcommittee. There were some in Congress who thought the answer to the problem of border security was just to increase personnel and inspections. That was the old model. The new model that I was advocating—and which forward-thinking Canadian business leaders like Perrin Beatty, head of the Canadian Alliance of Exporters, and Paul Tellier, president of Canadian National Railways, had been pushing—used a different approach. Instead of simply relying on more manpower at the border, the focus was on new technology. There had to be better intelligence gathering and sharing, as well as unified procedures and standards for processing people and freight arriving from abroad. I also wanted to push inspection and pre-clearance systems away from the actual crossing points to keep the border between us as seamless as possible.

Momentum toward this new model was building fast. The G–20 meeting of finance ministers and central bank governors took place in Ottawa in mid-November, two months after the terrorist attacks. Inevitably, the question of how to deal with terrorism that threatened the flow of commerce and global economic confidence and security

Paul Cellucci, age three, with fire truck, 1951. (*FAMILY PHOTO*)

Mr. and Mrs. Argeo R. Cellucci Jr., New York City, 1949. (*FAMILY PHOTO*)

Argeo R. Cellucci Jr., and Argeo L. Cellucci, with 1956 Oldsmobile. (*GRACEINGTON STUDIO, HUDSON, MA*)

Jan and Paul Cellucci on their wedding day, November 12, 1971. (*PHOTO BY CHUCK KERVKIUN*)

Vice President George Bush, Nancy Bush Ellis, Paul Cellucci and Kate Cellucci. Vice President tours Dirty Boston Hanger, 1988. (*JIM DAVIS*, THE BOSTON HERALD)

Lieutenant Governor–Elect Paul Cellucci with Ron Kaufman, election night, November 1990, Boston, Massachusetts. (THE BOSTON HERALD)

Massachusetts Secretary of Transportation Richard Taylor, US Secretary of Transportation Andy Card, Governor Bill Weld, Lieutenant Governor Paul Cellucci, Massachusetts Highway Commissioner Jim Kerasiotes, early stages of Boston's Big Dig, 1992.

John F. Kennedy
Library honors the
president. President
George H.W. Bush,
Caroline Kennedy,
Governor Paul
Cellucci, Boston,
Massachusetts, 1998.
(© *JOHN. F. KENNEDY*
LIBRARY FOUNDATION)

Governor Paul
Cellucci on campaign
trail, 1998.

Bob Yesue gives
Governor Paul
Cellucci a haircut
at Roc's Barbershop
and Hair Salon, 1997.

Governor George W. Bush and Governor Paul Cellucci, presidential campaign, Massachusetts, 2000.

The librarians Jan Cellucci and Laura Bush read to school children, 2000.

Israeli Minister of National Infrastructure Ariel Sharon, Governor Paul Cellucci and Governor George W. Bush, Jerusalem, 1998. (*FAMILY PHOTO*)

Governor Paul Cellucci with Colin Powell at Boston Red Sox game at Fenway Park, Boston, 1999. (© *1998 PHOTO BY CINDY LOO*)

Governor Paul Cellucci transfers powers to Governor Jane Swift at State House, Boston, April 10, 2001.

President George W. Bush tells Governor Paul Cellucci he will nominate him to be Ambassador to Canada, inauguration day, Washington, D.C, January 2001. (THE BOSTON HERALD)

President George W. Bush with Priscilla M. Cellucci in Rose Garden at White House, April 10, 2001. (*ANNE CELLUCCI*)

Jan Cellucci sheds tear with Ambassador Paul Cellucci at memorial on Parliament Hill, September 14, 2001. (*CP PHOTO/ TOM HANSON*)

Governor General Adrienne Clarkson, Prime Minister Jean Chrétien, and Ambassador Paul Cellucci at memorial service on Parliament Hill, September 14, 2001. (*PHOTO BY RAÚL ALFÉREZ*)

Progressive Conservative leader Joe Clark, Alliance leader Stockwell Day, NDP leader Alexa McDonough, Prime Minister Jean Chrétien, and Ambassador Paul Cellucci, at Ground Zero, New York City, September 29, 2001. (*CP PHOTO/ TOM HANSON*)

Judge Joseph Hart, Argeo Cellucci, Jr., New England Patriots' CEO Robert Kraft, Ambassador Paul Cellucci, and Bob Yesue, with Super Bowl trophy, Foxboro, Massachusetts, December 22, 2002. (© *NEW ENGLAND PATIOTS*)

United States Secretary of Homeland Security Tom Ridge, Foreign Minister John Manley, and Ambassador Paul Cellucci, in Ottawa for Smart Border Protocol, December 12, 2001. (*CP PHOTO/FRED CHARTRAND*)

Ambassador Paul Cellucci, Lieutenant Governor Myra Freeman of Nova Scotia, Jan Cellucci, and US Consul General (Halifax) Steve Kashket, about to board a helicopter to Sable Island, Nova Scotia, June 19, 2003.

was at the top of their agenda. Treasury Secretary Paul O'Neill arrived in Ottawa early so he could meet with Finance Minister Paul Martin. I met him at the airport and rode with him to the Chateau Laurier, discussing on the way the urgency of the border situation. The Chateau Laurier has a long history of being the venue for important political meetings and negotiations. I think it's fair to say that the meeting between O'Neill and Martin that day deserves to be considered in the category of policy turning points in the Canada–US relationship. It marked the formal beginning of the Smart Border process that has facilitated the movement of people and goods between our countries. "We are not only going to improve border crossing back to previous levels," said O'Neill, "but far surpass what we were able to do before September 11." And we were going to do this quickly. Martin and O'Neill agreed that the plan to accomplish this must be put in place as soon as possible. When they left the room to go to their G–20 meeting, those of us who remained behind started writing the Smart Border Action Plan. I remember actually dictating several of the action plan points right in that meeting as we got down to the hard task of working out the procedures and practical measures that would take the concept of a zone of confidence from the drawing board to reality. By the time Tom Ridge arrived in Ottawa on December 11, we had worked out the framework and much of the detail of the Smart Border Action Plan.

Thus was born at the Chateau Laurier a process that is still ongoing. Tom Ridge and Foreign Minister John Manley, who had been charged by the president and prime minister, respectively, to keep the border open to trade, tourism and legitimate travelers, did not just sign the Smart Border Action Plan in Ottawa that December 12, 2001. They committed themselves and their governments to a process that would make the border much more secure and more open. Ridge and Manley talked on the phone frequently and met every few months to discuss progress and set the agenda for agencies in both countries to put the plan together stage by stage. Their leadership was crucial in moving the Smart Borders Action Plan forward.

The Ridge–Manley process became the Ridge–McLellan process when Anne McLellan became deputy prime minister and minister for public safety and emergency preparedness, the counterpart to our secretary of homeland security. And when Michael Chertoff was named secretary of homeland security in 2005, this became the McLellan–Chertoff process. Secretary Chertoff's first foreign meeting was with Anne McLellan in Ottawa on March 17, 2005, the day before I departed my post at the embassy in Ottawa. For me there is particular satisfaction in the Smart Border Action Plan; it is considerably refined from its creation at the Chateau Laurier 2001, but like all vital and responsive public programs, it remains a work in progress.

Some of the urgency that drove the Smart Border discussions also rubbed off in another area of border business. In December 2004, Secretary Ridge and Minister McLellan met in Detroit to focus public attention on the need for a new crossing at the Detroit–Windsor corridor. We were absolutely convinced that this was the only way to escape gridlock in the future. The Smart Border approach—more people, better technology, free and secure trade (FAST)—was relatively easy when the political will was there to move things along. But building a new bridge or tunnel requires political will at all levels of government on both sides of the border. I was convinced that if we didn't reach a consensus on action in the near future, the gridlock that we all feared would become a reality.

To the relief of everyone, the border has not become the kind of bottleneck we feared. It was easy to imagine the kind of near-paralysis that would choke off the economic vitality to so many businesses and so many people on both sides of the border. For manufacturing, for tourism, for daily commuters on their way to work and for those who just want to visit friends and family, the Smart Border agreement has been enormously important. The border simply has not become an impediment. The Smart Border plan really is smart—special lanes for pre-cleared, regular border-crossers, new computer technology to record and track the movement of goods across the border. There are other parts of the agreement that are not visible but equally important. Principal among these is the much improved coordination and information-sharing among the policy and security agencies of both countries—the CIA, the FBI and the Department of Homeland Security, and the RCMP, CSIS and the Departments of Immigration and Justice on the Canadian side, and law enforcement at every level of government. One of the key provisions of the Smart Border Action Plan was the establishment of integrated border enforcement teams at key crossing points. There are sixteen of these, comprising law enforcement agencies from municipal, state and provincial, federal and in some cases even tribal governments. These agencies work together in teams using intelligence and law enforcement to stop criminals long before they get to the border.

I've said many times that only a small fraction of the people and goods that cross our shared border need close scrutiny. The idea behind the Smart Border is to get low-risk vehicles out of the line so that officials can concentrate on those vehicles that are high-risk or suspicious. By improving intelligence-sharing and law enforcement cooperation, we have been able to allow legitimate traffic to flow more smoothly and quickly. This is one of the great success stories of Canadian–American relations during my term as ambassador. It truly reflects the special relationship between our two countries and could only have been negotiated and implemented as quickly as it was because of the mutual trust between us and the determination everyone had to keep the special relationship working.

Less than two months after President Bush announced the US–led invasion of Afghanistan, I traveled with Prime Minister Chrétien and the Western provincial premiers on a Trade Canada West mission to Dallas and Los Angeles. My Canadian counterpart, Ambassador Michael Kergin was also part of this delegation, along with representatives from more than 100 Canadian companies. Team Canada trade missions had sometimes come in for criticism at home as being ineffective and a waste of taxpayers' dollars, but such criticism is off the mark. In the competitive global economy, companies and governments have to work continuously to hold on to what they have, let alone landing new contracts and investments. During my time as governor of Massachusetts I had led trade missions all over the world—Europe, Israel, Japan, China, Vietnam, Latin America and, of course, Canada. So I knew just how much of a positive economic impact such delegations can have.

Energy was the big issue when we were in Dallas. In addition to the formal roundtable talks that we had with Texas energy executives, we attended a state luncheon hosted by Governor Rick Perry and a performance of the world-renowned, Quebec-based Cirque du Soleil. Its three permanent shows in Las Vegas have entertained millions of Americans. And it started in Montreal, where it still trains performers and maintains its creative center under its founder, Guy Laliberté.

The dinners and formal meetings that are always part of a trade mission like this one are just the most visible part of the personal contacts that take place. The first morning in Dallas I got up early and took the elevator down to the exercise room for a workout on the treadmill. I would normally have preferred to jog outdoors, but the Canadian delegation had brought cold weather along to the American south. Alberta Premier Ralph Klein is, like me, religious about sticking to a daily exercise routine. He stepped on the treadmill next to mine and we started talking about the day ahead of us. A few minutes into our workout Aline Chrétien joined us on the treadmills. So there we had the Canadian government, the American government, and a major provincial government, side by side, facing in the same direction.

From Dallas we flew to Los Angeles and another round of meetings and formal events. I sat next to California Governor Gray Davis at the official state luncheon for our delegation. This was just a month before rolling black-outs and brown-outs hit the California power system. Governor Davis's popularity was already falling because of the state's faltering economy and high taxes; the power crisis pushed his popularity down into the critical zone. As a former governor who had faced the possibility of a serious energy crisis in my own state—where winter is a more serious matter than in most of California—I could commiserate with Davis. Although we belonged to different political parties and had different philosophies when it came to the role of government and taxation, I had always liked him. Davis is a fundamentally decent man and we always got along well at governors' meetings.

Happily, politics was not everything. That evening at a civic dinner I found myself seated next to one of Ottawa's favorite sons and another great Canadian cultural export, singer Paul Anka. I was delighted because, like everyone of my generation, I had grown up listening to Anka's songs on the Top 40 radio stations.

In addition to making valuable business contacts and exploring investment prospects, the trade mission was of immense personal value because I got time to talk to Prime Minister Chrétien; Pierre Pettigrew, the minister for international trade; the Western Canadian premiers; and Canada's ambassador to the United States, Michael Kergin. Over the next four years these were the people I would often see and with whom I would work. In getting to know them I felt that I was getting to know Canada even better. As old politicians, Prime Minister Chrétien and I would occasionally exchange war stories on the plane, him about campaigns in Quebec and across Canada and me about campaigns in Massachusetts and national campaigns across the US. With a couple of scotch and waters we had a good dialogue.

When our business was done in Los Angeles, Prime Minister Chrétien and I flew to New York City, to attend the "Canada Loves New York" rally at the Roseland Ballroom in Manhattan. We flew on the Canadian Forces Challenger jet that the prime minister uses for official travel, touching down at a small airfield in New Jersey. The next day was an unseasonably warm December day. The original idea for the rally came from Canadian Senator Jerry Grafstein and it was put together with the help of the prime minister's office, various Canadian government departments, and innumerable volunteers. Thousands of Canadians live in New York City, and it seemed as though all of them had turned out to watch the show. They were joined by thousands more who came to New York specifically for the rally. About 6,000 people crammed inside the Roseland Ballroom to listen to and watch Canadian performers Murray McLaughlan, Blue Rodeo, Edith Butler and Cirque du Soleil. Another 20,000 crowded outside on 53rd Street, watching the celebration of solidarity on a giant video screen. Pamela Wallin, one of Canada's favorite broadcasters, who later became Canada's consul-general in New York, was the emcee for what was a truly moving event.

The biggest ovation of the evening came when Pam introduced

Mayor Rudy Giuliani. His inspirational leadership in the days and weeks after 9/11 had made him "America's mayor" in the eyes of the world. The roar was deafening. "Thank you for coming here today," he said, "and I encourage you to spend every single penny you have!" Giuliani was presented with a magnificent original print by Canadian artist Charlie Pachter—best known for his imaginative and whimsical "moose art"—called "Side by Side." It depicted the Canadian and American flags blowing in the wind from a single flag pole. The image beautifully captured the spirit of solidarity that reigned that afternoon.

A few days after that rally, the government of Canada produced a beautiful Christmas present for the United States and the American people that year. It was a book of photos and personal reflections on how Canadians opened their homes and hearts to stranded Americans in the days following the terrorist attacks. Called A *Diary Between Friends*, this testament to friendship between our two nations had been produced by Heritage Canada. No one could be unmoved by the heartfelt sentiments expressed in that gift to the American people. So many stories and reflections in that book deserve to be mentioned. Here is just one, from the Dennis family of Decatur, Georgia; I think it captures the gratitude of Americans:

> While many Americans experienced only the evil, we were blessed to land among people who welcomed us with open arms, anticipating our every need. You taught thousands of people from all over the world how to care for strangers.

Prime Minister Chrétien presented me with a copy of A *Diary Between Friends* at a dramatic ceremony in the Parliament Buildings. Firefighters from New York and from cities across Canada were there.

The heroism of the hundreds of firefighters and policemen who entered the burning towers of the Trade Center, saving thousands of lives and losing their own, was known to everybody. I told the prime minister that I would personally present the copy of the book that he gave me to President Bush. A copy of A *Diary Between Friends* occupied a proud place in the Residence library for the rest of our time in Ottawa.

The spirit of cooperation between our countries was strong during those several months after 9/11. And the progress that we were making on the ground was, I think, equally impressive. One of the accomplishments in which I was involved was the opening of a new consulate in Winnipeg in December 2001. That brought to seven the number of US regional offices in Canada. The Winnipeg consulate is at the legendary corner of Portage and Main, so that every American consul at that post will know what the prairie wind feels like as it comes whipping through the city in January. My predecessor, Gordon Giffin, had done the difficult preparatory work in getting the State Department to approve this new American post. The State Department had closed the previous Winnipeg consulate as a cost-cutting measure back in 1986. This new office wasn't a full-service operation, which meant that visas, passports and immigration matters for the prairie region would still be taken care of by the Calgary consulate. But the fact of its opening reflected the importance that my government attached to economic relations with Manitoba and what we see as that province's prospect for growth. Our consul-general there, Todd Schwartz, continues to play an important public diplomacy role in Manitoba. Manitoba is a province with enormous hydro-electric potential in its northern watershed. That potential can't be developed without a significant and stable market. And that market would be mainly on our side of the border, exporting electricity to the power grids of such states as Minnesota, Wisconsin and Illinois.

Cutting the ribbon with me at the new Winnipeg consulate was Gary Doer, the premier of Manitoba. We had traveled together just a week before on the Team Canada West trade mission to Texas and California. Probably because of my years as a state lawmaker and governor, I feel a natural connection to provincial politicians. Gary and I got along well. I was impressed by his obvious perseverance; he led the New Democratic Party for three consecutive election defeats before finally leading it to victory in 1999. I like his pragmatic, fiscally responsible philosophy of governance, which confirmed my belief that state and provincial leaders tend to be problem-solvers and less ideological than their national counterparts. It seemed to me that if the NDP had room for a budget-balancing premier who even brought in tax cuts, it might actually have something to teach the Massachusetts Democratic Party!

Two days after opening the Winnipeg office, I gave a speech in Ottawa that really brought together the initiatives on which I had been working since becoming ambassador. Their importance was obviously immensely magnified by the terrorist attacks in September. My theme was the emergence of a North American community, pointing to the progress that NAFTA partners were making in integrating their economies for the mutual prosperity of their peoples. I repeated the message that I had delivered in Winnipeg, that we cannot be as dependent as we have been on foreign sources of energy. President Bush strongly believed that the answer was to build an integrated North American energy market that included Canada, the United States and Mexico. Coming from Winnipeg just the day before, where energy development had been center stage, I felt that this was an issue on which we had achieved some momentum.

The spirit of cooperation that existed when it came to border security and energy was also evident in the case of defense. Although reservations and criticisms were expressed by some, I sensed that most Canadians and their leaders appreciated the importance of Canada reinvesting in its military in order to maintain the proud and well-deserved reputation throughout the world of the Canadian forces.

The deployment of Canadian troops to Afghanistan in combat roles had raised some concerns in Canada. Critics said that this deployment differed from previous US–Canada joint operations because it placed Canadian troops under US operational control. That criticism was misguided. There was nothing unique about Canadian forces being under US operational control, or vice versa. We had been placing our troops under each other's operational control regularly for more than 50 years, since the founding of NATO and NORAD. In fact when the terrorists attacked on September 11, Canadian Air Force General Rick Findley was in command at Cheyenne Mountain, exercising operational control over NORAD's assets. When President Bush ordered a United States commercial airliner to be shot down on September 11, it was General Findley who scrambled the jet fighters in response to the president's order. As it happened, of course, the passengers took matters into their own hands and attacked the hijackers, so the ill-fated plane crashed in the fields of Pennsylvania rather than the White House or some other high profile target in Washington.

There is a significant distinction between operational control and command, a distinction that is vitally important from the standpoint of national sovereignty. Operational control means a commander has the ability to assign tasks to a nation's military forces, but does not decide exactly how they will accomplish those tasks. Nor does operational control give a field commander the right to order any nation's forces to perform tasks in contradiction to the laws and regulations of that country. In all cases where we, the United States and Canada, employ military forces, American troops remain under US command and Canadian troops remain under Canadian command. And that means that each nation is free to exert its command authority at any time, and withdraw from operational control if it sees fit.

That may sound like a merely technical distinction. But, in fact, it gets to the important question of who ultimately decides what a country's military will do and where it will be sent. From the beginning of my period as ambassador to Canada I was consistent in saying that if Canada joins the United States in a continental approach to security, Canadian sovereignty will not be infringed in any way. Canada will still have the option to send forces on UN peacekeeping missions in accordance with its national wishes. If the United States engages in an operation under the rubric of homeland security that Canada does not think is in its national interest, then Canada can simply decide not to participate.

The point that I tried to make to Canadians was that the idea of continental defense is not revolutionary, but evolutionary. Canada and the United States have been making plans for continental defense for a long time. Under the auspices of NORAD and NATO there are many existing defense plans. And together, our two militaries have drafted a Basic Security Document and a Combined Defence Plan that, along with existing NORAD procedures, form a framework for the defense of North America.

Canadian military capabilities are well known and valued by the United States. I would say again and again, however, that military capability must be sustained or it declines over time. That was why I took every opportunity to talk to Canadians about the need to increase their spending on defense. I was gratified that several key members of the Canadian government agreed that this was in Canada's best interest.

Our governments were working side by side in Afghanistan. The Smart Border Action Plan was being put in place, step by step. We had an ongoing dialogue on better integration of the energy market that had the active support of several of the premiers. In terms of the substance of the Canada–United States relationship, it was solid. Tangible signs of progress were evident on a number of fronts, although a lot of this was behind the scenes and at the level of officials where the media spotlight seldom shines.

There were, undeniably, some bumps in the road lying just ahead. They had much more to do with optics than the reality of the special relationship between our countries. Nevertheless, as the focus shifted toward Iraq, these bumps contributed to a sense that our relationship was entering difficult times.

CHAPTER SIX

Bumps in the Road

Cellucci (noun): A dressing-down or rebuke, as in "The boss gave me a Cellucci for losing the account." (from a *Globe and Mail* word challenge)

Early into my term as ambassador I discovered that the price of straight talk is that some people take offence. Critics opened the attack quickly. They accused me of "sermonizing," "hectoring," "bullying" and behaving in ways unsuited to a diplomat. One journalist described my style as "megaphone diplomacy." There began to creep into media coverage of my speeches and comments more and more references to me as a sort of proconsul or viceroy, "one of these tough guys sent out from Rome to straighten out the distant reaches of the empire," as the *Globe and Mail's* John Gray put it.

But I also quickly discovered that at least as many people—I think a majority of average Canadians—appreciated my straightforwardness. For every newspaper article or television commentary criticizing me there was one that praised me, for saying things that

Canadians needed to hear. And everywhere I went there were people who said, "Mr. Ambassador, I agree with you on that. You were right to say what you said."

I guess I should have known what to expect. From the day the first American ambassador presented his credentials to the governor general of the day, he probably bruised Canadian sensitivities and aroused suspicions. That goes with the turf today and that probably did then, too—the inevitable and inescapable occasional friction of Canadian–American relations. In the months after the invasion of Afghanistan, our relations went through some troubled times. These were bumps in the road—but only bumps. The relationship between the two countries is so fundamentally solid that it can survive occasional difficulties.

The week that the Canadian government presented me with a copy of A Diary Between Friends, another book arrived in local bookstores. It was John Ralston Saul's On Equilibrium. Saul is the husband of Governor General Adrienne Clarkson and a well-known Canadian essayist and novelist, with a reputation for being prickly and outspoken. The book caused a brief public flap, but nobody should have been surprised by his message. He described President Bush as "fragile" and "awkward" in the days after September 11; he painted a picture of the president that was unflattering and, as far as I was concerned, unrecognizable. Saul also argued that the West, particularly the United States, bore responsibility for the rise of Muslim militancy. Others have made that argument, so there was no particular novelty to it. Whether it was appropriate for someone bearing the title "His Excellency" and representing the Canadian state to be stirring these political waters was a matter best left to Canadians. My view, as I said it at the time, was that Saul was entitled to his minority opinion. I had traveled across much of Canada in the months after September 11 and I knew that Saul was out of step with the vast majority of Canadians. There are many bumps in the road of Canada–US relations, but the minor fuss over comments by someone like Saul do not really qualify as one.

The worst bumps are those that are sudden and unexpected. Jan and I had planned a dinner party at the Residence for some of the people who had been a great help to us during our first year in Ottawa. There were intimations of trouble early when Defence Minister Art Eggleton and Chief of the Defence Staff Ray Henault both called on their way to dinner, saying that they had to return to their offices. We had just sat down to dinner when the telephone calls started. First there was the State Department on the Residence line; then the cell phones of our guests started ringing. Almost all of the senior cabinet ministers were there, including Paul Martin, Bill Graham, John Manley and Anne McLellan. What was intended to be a pleasant first anniversary dinner to thank some of those who we had worked with and got to know during that first year became memorable in a way no one could have expected.

The telephone messages were all the same, all awful. Four Canadian paratroopers of the Princess Patricia's Canadian Light Infantry had been killed by fire from an American F-16 fighter jet. The four soldiers, Sergeant Marc Léger, Corporal Ainsworth Dyer, Private Nathan Smith and Private Richard Green, had been engaged in a nighttime live-fire exercise. The American pilot mistook the Canadians for enemy attackers. In the unfortunate jargon of such events, their deaths were the result of "friendly fire." The military investigations in both countries would go on for months. I thought then, and I still believe now, that this was the sort of disaster that happens in what the military calls the "fog of war."

The next morning President Bush telephoned Prime Minister Chrétien to express his condolences and promise to find out how this had happened. Later that afternoon I got a call from the *Globe and Mail's* Ottawa bureau asking me why the president had not made a public statement on the deaths of the four Canadians. I told him what the media already knew, that President Bush had immediately telephoned the prime minister and that a public statement of condolences would be issued soon. By that evening a written statement of condolences from the president was released. The next morning, I made a personal visit to Defence Minister Art Eggleton's office to express my personal sorrow and the sorrow of my government.

During the following days I consulted directly with top officials in the State Department and in the White House. I understood immediately how the resolve of the Canadian people would be sorely tested by this sad accident and how the pressure would mount on their government and the defense department to answer how and why this had happened. I worked closely with the embassy officers and military attachés and their Washington counterparts and superiors in order to craft appropriate responses. A joint inquiry, co-chaired by US Brigadier-General Stephen Sargeant and Canadian Brigadier-General Marc Dumais, was immediately established to investigate the accident. "As I told the prime minister," President Bush had said, "we will work together with Canada in a thorough and timely investigation to determine exactly how [this] tragedy in Afghanistan occurred." The inquiry was a concrete step toward fulfilling that promise.

Apparently this was not enough, at least in the eyes of some. A veritable firestorm of indignation burst from much of the Canadian media, in which the president's response was described as offhand, uncaring and inappropriate. This interpretation of President Bush's response to the accidental deaths of allied troops was staggeringly off the mark. It became clear that many of the critics expected an apology from my government. Our sincere and deeply felt sorrow and condolences were not enough. The president was expected to say "sorry."

An apology was not what the situation called for. At that point, none of us knew exactly how this friendly fire accident had happened. But military officers know that accidents—and sometimes fatal accidents—happen during combat. Condolences were in order and the president did the right and necessary thing in immediately calling the prime minister, followed by a formal statement issued by the White House several hours later.

Fortunately there were many Canadians, including family members of the slain soldiers, who also understood. Tina Scharples, the wife of a Canadian soldier, who attended the memorial service held in Edmonton, was among those who understood. "This is the whole purpose of why they joined," Tina said of the fallen soldiers. "It made me more proud to be Canadian. Our guys don't want to sit on the sidelines. This is what they trained for." I was at that moving memorial service, extending my personal condolences and the condolences of the president and the American people to the grieving families of the victims. In circumstances like these it never feels like enough, but I did my best to let them know that their pain and loss were understood and shared by all Americans.

Probably we should not have been surprised that the pain in Canada erupted occasionally in crowds booing the American national anthem at sporting events. The reality was that those instances were widely reported but rare. One such incident was at a hockey playoff game between the Vancouver Canucks and the Detroit Red Wings in late April of 2002. When I was asked to comment, I said that it was just the rude behavior of a small number of fans who in no way represented the feelings of the majority of

Canadians. There would be similar booing instances in Toronto and Montreal a year later, as temperatures rose over the war in Iraq. Such disrespect for the "Star Spangled Banner" was upsetting for Americans, but booing seemed an unworthy gesture when measured against the terrible sadness over the loss of those four lives.

What we did not know then was that the road of Canada–US relations would become much more bumpy before long.

That spring my embassy staff was busy with preparations for President Bush's visit to Canada for the G–8 Summit in Kananaskis, Alberta. As frequently happens in trying to set the agenda for such gatherings, we were all far from unanimous about what should be our priority concerns. In the case of Kananaskis, the United States seemed to be at odds with most of the other nations. The president felt the agenda should be centered on the problem of the conflict between Israel and the Palestinians; he believes that the promotion of democracy in the Middle East is crucial to the success of the war on terror. But as the date for the summit approached, it appeared to us that several of the G–8 leaders hoped to use the meetings to criticize my government's trade policies as being protectionist. Yet another concern came from the chair of this Canadian summit, Prime Minister Chrétien, who wanted the issue of aid to Africa to be at the top of the agenda. We agreed that Africa should be on the agenda but we strongly felt that the president's plan for the Middle East, which proposed the creation of a Palestinian state without Yasser Arafat at the helm, needed to be central to the leaders' discussions. Certainly there was no way that we were going to allow the president to be harangued by governments whose own track records on trade protectionism were far from spotless.

The day the president arrived in Calgary on Air Force One was one of those perfect summer days in Big Sky country. The skies were clear, the sunshine was brilliant, and the snow-capped Rockies lay gleaming on the western horizon. It's a Calgary tradition for distinguished visitors to put on a white Stetson for a photo on their arrival. This the president did quite gladly, immediately feeling at home in Canada's West. All of his fellow G–8 leaders followed suit except for French President Jacques Chirac, who refused to don his white cowboy hat. I guess President Chirac thought that the image of him in a Stetson, the favored hat of President Bush, might not play well at home.

I had dinner with President Bush, Condi Rice and Andy Card in the president's suite that evening. After dinner, we took a walk along a beautiful trail, just the four of us—and numerous security people. Over the next two days I sat in on the president's morning press briefings. President Bush's grasp of the issues once again impressed me deeply. I was proud to be a member of his team.

In the Canadian media's coverage of the Kananaskis Summit there was a lot of talk about the prime minister being at odds with the president, and suggestions that this reflected a lack of communication between the two leaders and between our two governments. This was becoming a familiar song, but it was simply not true. There was a profound difference between the optics and the reality of Canada–United States relations. The optics seemed to be all about conflict, disagreement and tension. The reality was continued cooperation and a significant progress on issues of mutual concern.

Just one day after the G-8 leaders left Kananaskis, while much of the media spotlight was focused on unfounded rumors of strained relations between the president and the prime minister, I joined Tom Ridge and John Manley in Niagara Falls for the signing one of the most important agreements in Canada–US relations in years. This was the formal adoption of the 30-point Smart Border declaration that had been agreed to on Tom's visit to Ottawa before Christmas.

We had been working hard for several months on the practical details of the agreement, which was so vital to the free flow of trade between our economies. But instead of paying attention to this positive development in Canada–US relations, some journalists seemed more concerned with whether Prime Minister Chrétien and President Bush liked each other.

Opposition leader Stephen Harper had raised this business of the personal chemistry at the top, saying that Prime Minister Chrétien had a lot to learn from the example of Prime Minister Brian Mulroney when it came to handling Canada's most important bilateral relationship. But I had been in meetings with President Bush and Prime Minister Chrétien and I knew that the chemistry was good and that they liked each other. The strains that existed in what was still, overall, an excellent relationship between our two countries had to do with various circumstances, not personalities.

If the road between our two countries was becoming less smooth, part of the reason may also have been that our national priorities were different. In the shadow of the terrorist attacks on the United States, national security and the fight against global terrorism were our number one priority, without any debate. I know that the Canadian government was taking the terrorist threat seriously, but I think that keeping the economy strong was probably higher on its scale of priorities. The United States had been attacked on its own soil, so it was natural that security would be our top priority. That said, if security wasn't Canada's top priority it was not far down the scale.

This difference between our national priorities influenced the reaction to my repeated calls for Canada to spend more on its military. When I was named ambassador, the only specific instructions that I received from Secretary of State Colin Powell was that I should talk to the Canadians about putting more money into defense. His instructions give a good idea of the concern in Washington about security and the concern about the state of the Canadian military. And that was why I had been talking about more military spending, almost from the day of my arrival in Ottawa. My government strongly believed that the war on terrorism might require military action against Saddam Hussein's Iraq. Along with the British we had intelligence information that convinced us that Saddam possessed weapons of mass destruction and that he was intent on producing more. On top of that there was the possibility that he would turn these weapons over to terrorists who would have no hesitation in using them against us. Instead of thousands of fatalities, as occurred on September 11, we would be looking at hundreds of thousands of deaths. The United States was not going to sit by and let that happen. We started to make the case to our allies and to the members of the coalition that went into Afghanistan that we might need a pre-emptive strike against Iraq. Obviously this was not something that we wanted to do on our own or that we thought we should have to do on our own. The president's first concern is the security of the United States and of Americans, but he firmly believed that the war against terror was vital to the security of freedom-loving peoples throughout the world.

As the specter of an attack against Iraq became imminent, my repeated calls for Canada to invest more in its own defense and in its military capabilities throughout the world became more urgent. My criticism was deliberate, but what I was saying about Canada's military was, in fact, mild compared to what some Canadians were saying. Canada's foremost military historian, Jack Granatstein, went on record saying that the Canadian Forces were literally on the verge of collapse. Even Deputy Prime Minister John Manley and Defence Minister John McCallum agreed with me that the Canadian military was under-funded. "I understand where they are coming from,"

Manley admitted. "The whole world looks to [the US] to do the heavy lifting and they think others should have the capability to play a bigger role in that. Maybe they have a point."

But when I delivered the same message the reception was sometimes a bit frosty. Despite the fact that several members of the Canadian government publicly expressed their agreement with me, as did leading members of the Canadian Forces, I was accused by some of meddling in Canadian affairs and proposing something that would threaten Canadian sovereignty. The meddling charge was, I thought, unfair. It makes sense for two countries who inhabit the same continent and who are joined economically to be working together on security issues. Canada and the United States have been doing precisely that since World War II. That's what NORAD is all about. Too few people realize that a Canadian general was in command at NORAD headquarters on the day the terrorists attacked America. It was only natural, I thought, to suggest that our interests were inseparable. My message was always the same. The United States cannot defend the North American continent alone. We need Canada's help. Canada occupies a huge piece of territory in North America and we need Canada's cooperation in defending the air, the land and the sea. When it comes to security, our backyards have no fence that would be respected by those who seek to do us harm.

Canadian sovereignty? Every time I would talk about the need for the Canadian government to spend more on its military there were those who said that this would be at the expense of Canadian sovereignty. I never understood the logic of these concerns. What could give a greater boost to Canadian sovereignty than spending enough to take care of its own defense? National security doesn't just happen. Someone has to pay for it. Those Canadians who imagined that they were protecting their national sovereignty by permitting the United

States to take care of an increasing share of continental defense had the equation backward. I was determined to push hard on this issue. I knew that my government expected me to and I knew that it was important, for both of our countries. I told Canadians that we were concerned about Canada's troop strength, which had declined to levels that jeopardized the military's ability to maintain existing commitments, let alone take on new ones. How many Canadians knew that when the initial six-month deployment of 850 Canadian troops to Afghanistan ended in the summer of 2002, it could not be replaced because there were not the troops or support resources to do so? Although, after an operational pause of one year, Canada commanded the Kabul multinational brigade for the International Security Assistance Force (ISAF) from August 2003 to August 2004 (supplying much of the staff and a reinforced, mechanized infantry battalion), total strength during the first six months was 2200 personnel—primarily from the Royal Canadian Regiment based in Petawawa, Ontario—and 2300 personnel during the second six months—primarily from the Royal 22nd Regiment based in Valcartier, Quebec. This total of 4500 soldiers over a twelve-month period represented more than 40 percent of Canada's deployable forces in Afghanistan. We were also worried about what military people call interoperability. Quite simply, the Canadian government needed to invest in military hardware, including the sophisticated electronic and computer technology that a modern military relies on. Although the naval vessels of the two counties had a high degree of interoperability, there were major problems with Canadian forces on land and in the air: they could not coordinate their activities with those of their US counterparts. And we were also concerned about strategic lift capability. Canadians had to rely on others, including the United States, to transport troops and equipment to trouble spots around the world.

I think some people were still living under the post–Cold War illusion that there would be a peace dividend because the world was now a safer place. It wasn't, and the terrorist assault on September 11 had demonstrated what my government believed was the tip of the iceberg—the real potential for mass slaughter by terrorist groups and rogue states. Those Canadian political and opinion leaders who apparently believed that security could be purchased at home and abroad without paying a price were doing Canada an enormous dis-service. And it wasn't just my government that felt this way. As the temperature rose on the military spending debate, I pointed out that the French government had recently announced a 36 percent increase in defense spending. Apparently the French believed that there was more to security than "soft power." Why some Canadian leaders did not see that was beyond me.

President Bush himself stepped directly into the debate at a NATO meeting in Prague, when he called on all NATO members to increase their defense spending. He warned that the threat posed by terrorists and terrorist states is real and that every free nation is a potential target. The president did not mention Canada specifi-cally, but after my repeated warnings over the previous year, nobody in Ottawa could miss the message. But not everybody appreciated the message. Defence Minister John McCallum, who only weeks before had been calling for a big infusion of new money for the Canadian military, apparently thought my government had crossed the line. "I would not urge the president of the United States or the US ambassador to Canada to do my job to ask for more defense spending," he said. "I think this is a Canadian matter.... It is a made-in-Canada decision, so while Mr. Bush may be asking for what I'm asking for, I'm not asking for his help." McCallum went on to say that some Canadians—and I assume that he counted himself among them—were "ticked off" by my public statements on the military spending issue.

Such a rebuke by a Canadian cabinet minister to the president and me would normally have been the major news item in the Canadian media. But McCallum was overshadowed by reports that the prime minister's director of communications, Françoise Ducros, had called President Bush a moron. She made the comment to a Canadian journalist during a discussion of the president's efforts to convince NATO members that a military strike against Saddam Hussein might be necessary and should be the alliance's number one concern. The moron comment became a major news story in Canada and even received mention on cable news channels and talk radio in the States. Some opposition politicians in Canada called on the prime minister to fire Ducros, but within days she did the job herself, submitting her resignation.

I think the whole episode was blown way out of proportion by some members of the press who tried to use it as confirmation of their belief that the president and the prime minister did not like or respect each other. Prime Minister Chrétien did state that he felt Ducros's comment was inappropriate. But many people did not think the prime minister had gone far enough or fast enough. Former Prime Minister Brian Mulroney, a good friend of the president's father, wrote an open letter to Canadian newspapers in which he said that the incident had damaged Canada–United States relations. Mulroney met with President Bush, along with Dick Cheney, Condi Rice and my close friend Andy Card, in the Oval Office after Ducros's rather juvenile outburst. Some people said that Mulroney was doing what Prime Minister Chrétien should have done, reassuring the White House about the fundamental soundness of our bilateral relationship and the goodwill that most Canadians felt toward the United States.

The bumps in the road were not ended. Indeed, the bump involving Maher Arar was one of the most difficult that we faced in my four years in Ottawa. And to this day I believe the US government complied with all international law and all and treaty obligations in deporting Arar from the United States to Syria. The view of Canadian critics is that the deportation of Arar to Syria was an infringement of Canadian sovereignty. Arar was a software engineer living in Montreal. He held Syrian citizenship from birth and acquired Canadian citizenship after immigrating when he was a teenager. On a return flight from Switzerland Arar was detained at JFK Airport in New York. He was questioned there, based partially on information that had been provided to the US by Canadian authorities in our normal exchange of information. Arar had been the target of police investigations in Canada for some time, because of suspected links to al Qaeda. The result was that he was kept in New York for two weeks and then deported to his native Syria, where he was still a citizen, on October 10, 2002. Arar's deportation became a lightning rod for the Canadian media's preoccupation with any signs of strain in the Canada–US relationship. My government was accused of disregarding Canadian sovereignty by deporting to a third country a Canadian citizen who was traveling on a Canadian passport. Another issue regarding Arar was whether anyone in the Canadian government had acquiesced or supported his deportation to Syria. After a thorough investigation, we were able to tell the Canadian government that the decision to deport Arar to Syria was made by United States officials alone, without any input from anyone in the Canadian government.

This was the first and only time that I had to deal with a formal protest from the Canadian government. Minister of Foreign Affairs Bill Graham publicly expressed his indignation that a Canadian citizen had been deported without the Canadian government being informed. Following this protest, the United States and Canadian governments exchanged letters, in which each undertook to notify the other country if either government was going to remove involuntarily a national of the other country to a third country. At the same time each country retains all rights to do what is in its security interest. As a practical matter, I believe this makes it unlikely that anything like the Arar situation would happen again.

Arar was eventually returned to Canada. He was later chosen *Time Canada*'s "newsmaker of the year" for 2004, which only proves there are many ways to make news. Many Canadians prefer to see the Arar case as an issue about Canadian sovereignty. I continue to believe, however, that his arrest and deportation were justified given the information that was available and the threat of global terrorism.

On his first visit to President Bush's ranch in Texas, about a week after I stepped down as ambassador to Canada, Prime Minister Paul Martin remarked that the most surprising thing about the Canada–United States relationship is that we don't disagree more often. I couldn't agree more. This was the point that I made over and over as I crossed Canada, giving speeches, appearing on radio call-in shows and giving interviews. Sure, there are occasional bumps in the road, and there were a spate of them in 2002. But these conflicts needed to be put in perspective and judged against the larger backdrop of massive cooperation and goodwill on most issues.

It is worth reminding ourselves just how exceptional our relationship is. The Canada–US trading relationship is the largest in the history of the world, at about $500 billion per year or roughly $1.4 billion per day. The value of trade that crosses the Ambassador Bridge between Windsor and Detroit—a single crossing point—is greater than the total value of trade between the United States and Japan. Millions of jobs on both sides of the border are dependent on this trade. Families depend on it to put food on the table and to maintain their living standards. In order to continue this relationship, goods, investment and people must be able to move freely, fairly and smoothly. The Canada–US Free Trade Agreement and NAFTA have been great successes, but with this large a trading relationship there are bound to be occasional sources of friction. Trying to resolve them was one of my main roles as ambassador.

When I arrived in Canada in April 2001, one of my first briefings was on the Prince Edward Island potato wart. That may not seem like the dizzying heights of international diplomacy, but potatoes are PEI's chief export, and much of the province's potato production finds its way to the United States. So when a fungus started to go through some of the province's potato fields, the USDA imposed an import ban. The US agricultural officials have a legislative responsibility to protect our agricultural sector from disease, and that's what they were doing.

Canada's agricultural scientists and politicians addressed this problem right away, knowing how important potato exports were to the PEI economy. By the time I was briefed on the issue, the scientific evidence was clear: the fungus had been brought under control and posed no threat to potato crops in the United States. I was convinced that my government should lift the ban. The fact that the president was arriving in Quebec City for the Summit of the Americas gave me an additional incentive to try to get this issue resolved before he met with Prime Minister Chrétien. Unfortunately, even when the science is clear, it takes time to move the bureaucracy.

We could not get the USDA to lift the ban in time for the president's visit, even though I knew it would not be long before trucks of PEI potatoes would be heading south across the border again. In fact, the ban was lifted just two months later. In the meantime, though, Prime Minister Chrétien seemed to take great pleasure in serving PEI potatoes to the president at every meal during the Quebec City summit.

One dispute that seems to have gone on forever involves softwood lumber. I soon discovered that this issue is poorly understood and often misrepresented. The conflict is rooted in the historically and fundamentally different systems of harvesting lumber. In the United States, most of the land where logging takes place is privately owned. In Canada, most forest resources are Crown land that is under the control of the provinces. The provincial premiers hold great power when it comes to natural resources. There have been times in the past when, in British Columbia, the premier would drop the stumpage fee—the tax per harvested tree that a logging company has to pay the province—in order to keep provincial lumber mills open and workers on the job during a down time. My government has always maintained that the stumpage fee system, which does not require logging companies to go to the expense of purchasing or leasing the land from which they harvest trees, is an unfair subsidy. So we have had negotiations for decades, and a series of short-term agreements, without any clear resolution of the issue. Things are made even more complex by the fact that each province sets its own rules and policies. This makes Ottawa's job in negotiating an agreement even more difficult. The last short term agreement expired in 2001 and we started immediately trying to work out a long-term solution. We thought that we had reached a breakthrough in 2003, but that came unraveled because of the objections of some provinces. However, I'm hopeful that we have agreement on a road map that will eventually lead to a resolution where everyone is satisfied that market forces set the price of lumber.

The other challenge that we face in resolving this issue—and one whose importance shouldn't be minimized—involves our very different systems of government. I was present at a meeting at the Oval Office between the president and Prime Minister Chrétien in 2002. Softwood lumber negotiations were underway in Washington that very day. Both the president and the prime minister thought it would be a good idea to make a public expression of optimism on these talks, saying, "We've told our negotiators to sharpen their pencils." I told them that I didn't think this was advisable, but in the end I was overruled. The problem that I foresaw was that this sort of message means something very different in the Canadian and American systems of government. In Canada, it is a clear message to negotiators to get the deal done. Policy-making is much more centralized in Canada and when the prime minister is determined that something be done, providing his party has a majority in the Commons, it will get done. This is not true in the United States because of the division of powers and the independence of Congress from the executive branch. The president's wishes are often stymied in Congress. So when those negotiations failed, there was some bitterness in Canada. I understood these feelings, but Canadians were wrong to blame the president. He genuinely wanted to see the issue resolved. And I still think it can be resolved. Part of the problem has become that the two sides have been sparring on this issue for so long that they don't know how to end the fight. It's a bit like a family feud that keeps going by its own momentum, long after it is clear that both countries would be better off if it were ended. But the goal line is in sight and what remains is to continue to push, on both sides, until we cross that line.

Conflicts are generally understood as signs of failure. My experience has been that this is not necessarily so. I think the case of bovine spongiform encephalopathy (BSE) or "mad cow disease" as it is widely known, demonstrates this. When Canadian Minister of Agriculture Lyle Van Cleef called to let me know that a confirmed case of BSE had been discovered in Alberta in May 2003, I knew that this would have a huge impact on the cattle industry, an industry that is highly integrated across the Canada–United States border. For the next two years, BSE remained a major issue, with economic harm suffered on both sides of the border. In the end, though, I believe that the actions taken by our two governments will be remembered as an important example of how two nations can, and must, work together to solve difficult problems.

After a lot of cooperation at all levels, from scientists to policy-makers, we took a big step toward reopening the US border to live Canadian cattle when the so-called Minimal Risk Rule was to be implemented by the USDA on March 7, 2005. It involves a science-based system of checks and monitoring to ensure that the risk of imported beef being infected with BSE is a minimal as possible. Canada was the first minimal risk region under this USDA rule. Despite the strong support of the president and the USDA for ending the ban on live Canadian cattle, a US federal district court judge issued an injunction that blocked the lifting of the ban. But this was just a temporary setback. The science is clear, the system put in place by the USDA and complied with to the letter by Canadian producers is strong, and I expected when I stepped down as ambassador that Canadian cattle would soon be heading to packing plants in the United States.

What started as a health issue, and should have remained a health issue, became seen as a trade conflict. This was unfortunate and it certainly prevented the matter from being resolved more quickly. People and companies suffered in both countries. Canadian cattle farmers don't need to be reminded about the hundreds of millions of dollars they lost during the import ban. But there were losses on the American side too. Many American packing plants had to lay off workers because without supply from Canada they couldn't find enough cattle to slaughter. So there was hardship on both sides of the border. But in the long run, all the careful steps we took and the industry rules that we put in place will pay off in improved public trust in our integrated food supply. The professional manner in which authorities in Canada and the United States addressed the issue showed the real benefits of Canadian–American cooperation.

I also know that the Canadian press portrayed trade disputes as one-sided with the US as the heavy. You rarely heard about the above-quota tariffs that Canada imposed on our many dairy and poultry products coming from the US. And of course Canada takes siginificant measures to protect its culture, although with Cirque de Soleil dominating Las Vegas, Celine Dion, Dan Aykroyd, Natalie MacMaster, and so many others, it's hard to believe the protection is needed. Canada's artistic talent is diverse and deep. Its culture is unique and strong. I'll give just one example of where I don't think the protections are working. When I returned home to Massachusetts, I went to Farina Chrysler in Marlboro and ordered a Chrysler 300 with a satellite radio. Satellite radio is a new technology where you can tune into over 100 channels of commercial-free stations offering music, news, entertainment and sports including play-by-play of NHL games (if they ever start playing again). It has been available in the United States for several years. When Jan purchased her Yukon Denali in Canada two years ago, we learned that satellite radio was not yet available in Canada, and it would not be available until "Canadian content" issues could be addressed. What's more Canadian than hockey? Millions of Canadians have been denied this entertainment option. I know it's on its way to resolution, but here's the irony: My Chrysler 300 was built in Brampton, Ontario, and shipped to the United States with the satellite radio.

––––––––––––––

Show me a case of two countries that never disagree and I'll show you a case of two countries that have little to do with each other. Canada and the United States are two countries that have a lot to do with each other, and so it is inevitable that friction arises in their relations from time to time. My regular reassurances that the overall Canada–US relationship was excellent, from the top down, was dismissed by some as overly optimistic. But I firmly believed this to be true, despite what naysayers thought. Conflict, confrontation and disagreement always seem to be more newsworthy than cooperation and agreement. I knew that, and so I wasn't surprised or worried when some in the media seemed preoccupied with the friction and overlooked the cooperation.

But disagreements can and do arise, even between the best of friends. The war in Iraq was one of these.

CHAPTER SEVEN

Security Trumps Trade

I was new to diplomacy when I went to Ottawa, but I was not so naive that I did not expect there would be no disappointments along the way. But to this day I am painfully disappointed that the Canadian government did not participate in the invasion of Iraq. I thought the decision was wrong and I thought that, with leadership from the government, the Canadian people would have been proud to see their troops as part of the coalition against Saddam Hussein. Instead of leadership, there was indecision, mixed signals and confusion. One Canadian journalist said that reading Ottawa's position on the Iraq issue required the skills of a séance master and the deductive powers of a Sherlock Holmes. Very true, and I think that even some of the senior members of the cabinet could not figure out what was going on.

For those who were watching events in Ottawa at the time, the Canadian decision to stay out of the war in Iraq was not entirely a surprise. There had been disquieting warning signs. For months, Prime Minister Chrétien had been insisting that the Iraq problem should be settled through the United Nations, that any military intervention must have the sanction of the world body. Of course that was what President Bush and Secretary of State Colin Powell had been trying to accomplish. Only when the UN's Security Council was unable to act did the United States start to put together a broad coalition of nations that would finally confront the problem of Saddam Hussein. Whatever the opposition of France and other governments, the US was not prepared to tolerate the threat from Iraq.

I wanted Canada to be part of the coalition against Saddam, but I knew that it would be an uphill battle to convince the government to come on board. For the US, regime change in Iraq—getting rid of Saddam—was an important part of the war on terror. I think there were some in the Canadian government who agreed with us, and we had support on the Alliance and Conservative benches. But in the end the prime minister and his government took the position that Saddam Hussein's Iraq was like a lot of other nasty, oppressive regimes throughout the world. The prime minister's question was, "Where do you draw the line?" In other words, Why single out Iraq when there are many other vicious and potentially dangerous regimes?

I had talked to enough Canadians and appeared on enough radio call-in programs to know that there was real division among the Canadian people about whether their country should join the coalition. There was also division among Americans. But leaders lead by moving public opinion in a direction they believe is right. That is what George W. Bush did; that is what Tony Blair did in Britain, where the population was as divided on the issue of war in Iraq as Canadians were. In fact, Blair's position was more precarious than that of Prime Minister Chrétien, because large parts of his own Labour Party were opposed to the war. But Blair took the risk and went to the British public and made the case for invading Saddam's Iraq. Jean Chrétien obviously decided to lead Canada in a different direction.

In the weeks before the invasion, the mood of the government was becoming apparent. First there was the Françoise Ducros "moron" remark. Less significant than the remark itself was the fact that her boss did not immediately and publicly rebuke her, if for nothing else than her inexcusable rudeness. Then came Carolyn Parrish, the Liberal MP who caught the attention of reporters with "Damn Americans! I hate those bastards!" Once more, there were demands that the prime minister let everyone know that the comments were unacceptable. Chrétien did allow that he thought the comment was not appropriate, but he rejected opposition demands that Parrish be disciplined. At a time of particular uneasiness in the relations between Ottawa and Washington, the prime minister did not take steps to lower the level of tension.

One of the ironies in this affair was that Parrish represents the constituency of Mississauga, which may have a greater number of Canadian subsidiaries of US–based companies than any riding in Canada. In fact, Parrish sent me a letter of apology a few days later and there are no hard feelings between us. But emotions were running high, and when that happens people sometimes say things that they don't mean—or at least that they don't mean to say. The two of us actually had some fun with the whole episode later at the annual Parliamentary Press Gallery dinner. Parrish and I appeared in a short video based on Martin Scorsese's film *Taxi Driver*. I did my Robert De Niro imitation, driving up to Parliament in a cab muttering, "Canadians. Canadians everywhere. Saying bad things about Americans." Parrish flags me down, gets in and says, "Driver, I want to go to the left; the far left." "Are you talkin' to me?" I answer. "This taxi only goes to the right; the far right." Those at the press gallery—journalists, politicians, aides, and political activists—loved it and we had fun making it. The video was a light interlude during a tense time.

For the United States, the question of Iraq was clear. Saddam and his government had failed to comply with the terms of UN resolutions passed after the 1991 Gulf War. We knew that Saddam Hussein had possessed and used weapons of mass destruction in the past, killing thousands of Kurds with poison gas. And we had evidence that strongly suggested to us that his regime was doing everything in its power to acquire more weapons of mass destruction and possibly nuclear weapons. Even if Saddam did not intend to use such weapons, we believed that, given his track record, he would be quite prepared to give them to terrorist groups who might use them against the United States, Israel or some other country. Saddam had shown that he was not serious about complying with UN disarmament orders and cooperating with weapons inspectors. He played a game of chicken in which he would let in inspectors only when the US government turned up the heat in the Security Council. In the world that existed after September 11, the United States was not prepared to be hit before we hit back; so we thought Saddam's regime had to be destroyed.

One of the myths surrounding the lead-up to the war in Iraq is that my government acted unilaterally, without regard for the views of other nations. The reality is just the opposite. We tried repeatedly to work through the UN Security Council. The president and Secretary Powell had addressed the UN and NATO, pointing to Iraq's violations of UN resolutions and warning that the danger posed by Saddam's regime justified a military intervention. There was already one UN resolution authorizing the use of force if Iraq was found to be in non-compliance with UN orders, which it certainly was. But for various reasons some members of the Security Council insisted that there must be a second resolution authorizing military action. That was just a way to put off the day of reckoning. France made clear that it would not vote for any new resolution calling for the use of military force against Iraq and managed to persuade Germany and Russia to join it in blocking any action by the Security Council. The fact of the matter is that the president had indeed tried to work through the UN, only to find that the Security Council was paralyzed by the French-led opposition to regime change in Iraq.

Despite the obvious hesitations about the prospect of an invasion, we believed that Canada would be with us even without a second UN resolution on Iraq. We knew that the Canadian government wanted a new resolution and that it worked hard to get one through the Security Council. But it was not to be. It was in the House of Commons that Prime Minister Chrétien announced that Canada would not join the coalition. For those of us who had worked so hard to persuade Canadians on the Iraq question, it was a truly bitter dis-appointment—particularly the sight of Liberal ministers and backbenchers standing to cheer his announcement.

On March 19, President Bush announced that coalition troops had begun their invasion of Iraq. I was in Denver, stuck in a huge snowstorm. I had been in the command center of NORAD at Colorado Springs when I was advised that I should leave immediately if I wanted to leave ahead of the snowstorm. Jan and I were rushed to the Colorado Springs airport and managed to get off the ground before the storm hit, but we got only as far as Denver. All flights were grounded for two very frustrating days. Things were happening back in Ottawa and I needed to get back.

After Jean Chrétien announced that Canada would not join the coalition invasion of Iraq, the Canadian government tried to soften the blow. My embassy received assurances at a meeting at the Department of Foreign Affairs and International Trade that, although Canada would not participate as an active partner in the war coalition, once the war began the government would say positive things about the United States and negative things about Iraq. Ottawa promised to keep its naval vessels in the Persian Gulf and any Canadian military personnel already assigned to US or British units going into Iraq would remain with those units. So I was surprised when, the day after coalition troops began their assault, the Canadian government took a more critical line than I had been led to expect. Instead of saying much that was positive about my government and its decision to go to war, Prime Minister Chrétien chose to emphasize the need for any such military action to be authorized by the UN. There was a suggestion—intentional or not—that what the US-led coalition was doing in Iraq lacked legitimacy.

Stranded in Denver, trying to keep up with what was happening via cell phone, was bad enough. When I heard that Minister of Natural Resources Herb Dhaliwal had described President Bush as a failed statesman, I went from frustration to anger. If there was a failure of statesmanship in this whole affair it was on the part of France: President Jacques Chirac and his foreign minister, Dominique de Villepin. They had used France's permanent seat on the Security Council to block necessary steps against a regime that had shown itself to be a danger to its neighbors and its own people and that had the potential to pose an even larger threat. So I was angry with Dhaliwal and I fully expected that he would be rebuked by Prime Minister Chrétien. Think about how the Canadian government and the Canadian media would react if a US cabinet officer criticized the prime minister as Dhaliwal did the president of the United States? I know the answer and I'm sure most Canadians do too. There would be outrage. People would want to know that the person at the top did not condone the public expression of such sentiments. I understand that Chrétien was displeased with Dhaliwal's remark, but if there was any rebuke, it was behind closed doors. The prime minister had refused to react strongly to what had become a string of insulting comments from his own Liberal colleagues, and that gave the impression that he didn't take them all that seriously. I thought the Ducros and Parrish remarks could possibly be dismissed as emotional outbursts that didn't amount to much. But Dhaliwal was the senior cabinet minister from British Columbia and his comment carried considerably more weight. Premier Klein of Alberta received a stern rebuke from the Canadian government for sending me a letter thanking the United States for "its leadership in the war on terrorism and tyranny," while Dhaliwal's insult to the President went unchallenged and uncriticized? What was I to think?

Ralph Klein was not the only premier to publicly express his support for my government in Iraq, although he was the only one to receive a public dressing-down from the federal government. Premier Ernie Eves of Ontario had gone even further. At a rally in Toronto he spoke of how our countries had been allies and friends for decades. "To be frank," he said, "Americans have really been responsible for defending this country, in large part, over those many decades. We have not seen clear to devote the resources that are necessary to have armed forces of our own that are able to entirely defend, on their own strength, this country in the event of war." British Columbia Premier Gordon Campbell echoed his comments, saying that Canadians sit "at the safety of the doorstep of the United States."

As I thought back on the days and weeks following the terrorist attacks on September 11, and the solidarity that had existed between our governments, I was saddened by the rift that had developed between us on the crucial issue of Iraq. I was not the only one. The day before I was scheduled to give a speech to the Economic Club of Toronto, a week after the invasion, I called Condi Rice at the White

House and advised her on what I was planning to say the next day. She agreed that it was the right thing to do.

That day I sat down with the text of the speech that I planned to give in Toronto. I put it in bullet form to keep my focus firmly on the points that I wanted to make. I would start with some observations that I often made about the economic ties between our countries. Then I would address the questions that were on everyone's mind: what was going on in the Canada–United States relationship and what did my government think about Canada's decision to stay on the sidelines in the war in Iraq? I knew that this would be the most important, and possibly the most controversial, act of public diplomacy in my two years on the job. I wanted to get it right.

I had spoken to many groups across Canada in my two years on the job, but the mood that day in Toronto was different. There was a palpable sense of expectation and a feeling that things were not right in the Canada–US relationship. I could have made soothing remarks about our relations and I could have offered a few comforting platitudes about friendship and shared values. But this was an occasion for something more direct. I was going to deliver the message that my government thought the people of Canada ought to hear, the straight and unvarnished truth. About five minutes into my speech I turned to the war on terror. I talked about the cooperation between our governments on security issues, including the border, intelligence sharing and more common immigration policies. I reminded everyone that the person in command of NORAD on September 11, 2001, when military jets were scrambled to shoot down a commercial United States airline, was a Canadian general. And I talked about Canada's valuable combat contribution in Afghanistan.

Then I got to the heart of the matter. There was disappointment in Washington and elsewhere, in the United States, I said, that

Canada was not supporting us fully in Iraq. Like Canada, we very much wanted the United Nations to be a relevant and effective body. But once those efforts failed, we no longer saw things from a multi-lateral perspective. For us, it had become much more basic than that. It was about family. My voice was rising at this point, not in anger but from a passion born of my conviction that a wrong decision had been made. There is no security threat to Canada, I said, that the United States would not be ready, willing and able to help with. There would be no debate. There would be no hesitation. We would be there for Canada, part of our family. That was why so many in the United States were disappointed and upset that Canada was not supporting us fully in Iraq.

This turned out to be the diplomatic equivalent of a bombshell. Many Canadians appreciated the candor. There were others who misunderstood the tone and intent of my remarks. One journalist went so far as to refer to me as a "hired thug" making "veiled threats." This was nonsense. I wanted Canadians to know what my govern-ment thought, and now they knew. This was an important act of public diplomacy.

During the question-and-answer session after the Toronto speech, someone asked me about continuing delays at the bridges between Canada and the United States and their effect on commerce. My answer was straightforward: Security trumps trade. This was the first time that I expressed it as simply as that, but I had been communi-cating this same message for a year and a half. My government and the American people saw security as our number one priority. Trade and economic security were obviously vitally important to us, but everything took a back seat to our physical security.

I think this is what some people in the Canadian government did not fully appreciate. My government saw Iraq as an issue of national security. It was a vital part of the war on terror. Those who said, "Well, Saddam didn't bring down the World Trade Center," misunderstood the nature of the global terrorism threat. It didn't come from just al Qaeda and the Taliban. It came from all those groups and states that were prepared to use terror and weapons of mass destruction to threaten peace and harm freedom-loving nations throughout the world. Iraq was not a different war from Afghanistan. It was a different front in the same war on international terrorism and the rogue states that supported it.

The Canadian government took the position that these were two different wars. Prime Minister Chrétien made a number of statements in which he differentiated between Canadian troops who were in Afghanistan to assist in the war on terror, and what he called regime change in Iraq. The point that I tried to get across on behalf of my government was that regime change in Iraq was about combating terror. The possibility of Saddam turning over weapons of mass destruction to terrorists was a direct threat to the security of the United States and its people. Our coalition in Iraq was there to destroy an evil regime that had invaded its neighbors, engaged in the mass slaughter of its own people, used weapons of mass destruction, defied the United Nations on numerous occasions and for a long time destabilized the entire Middle East. If this wasn't an indictment deserving of military intervention then I don't know what would be. Tony Blair saw it that way, as did John Howard of Australia, Silvio Berlusconi of Italy, Jose-Maria Aznar of Spain and several other important world leaders.

I have always been puzzled that the Chrétien government would try to suggest that Canada could not become involved in a war to remove Saddam without clear UN authorization. Where was the UN authorization when Canada participated in the attacks on Kosovo, helping to stop the genocide there and bring down the Milosovic regime in Yugoslavia? Of course there was no UN authorization. The UN had refused to authorize military action to stop the ethnic cleansing, so NATO stepped in and did what had to be done. Now, a few years later, the Canadian government took the position that there could be no war without UN blessing.

When I expressed my disappointment that "Canada is not there for us now," I was talking about the Canadian government. I knew that many Canadians shared my disappointment and I firmly believed that if their government had decided to explain to its citizens why Canada should stand shoulder to shoulder with the United States on Iraq, as Tony Blair had done in Britain, then Canadian public opinion would have been even more supportive of my government. Canadians had heard a litany of insults, criticisms and reasons why Canada should not support war against Iraq. And despite a heavy barrage of anti-Americanism in the media during the months leading up to the invasion of Iraq and the ouster of Saddam, polls showed that most Canadians expected that their country would stand with us and were willing to accept their country's participation in this phase of the war on terror.

What I said in the Toronto speech needed to be said. I thought it was important that the Canadian people understood that my government's disappointment at not being able to count on its neighbor and greatest friend was deep and real. I knew that Canadians were at loggerheads with one another over their government's decision to sit out the war. For example, when Don Cherry and Ron MacLean used *Hockey Night in Canada*'s "Coach's Corner" for an impassioned conversation about the Iraq war and Canada, bumping all talk of hockey to the side, it was clear that the temperature was high. I thought it was time to bring it down a few degrees. The disappointment felt by my government over Canada's decision was just that—disappointment. It was nothing like the anger that we felt toward the French and the Germans for effectively torpedoing efforts to force Iraq to comply with the UN's disarmament resolution. It was easy for the French and Germans to preach a policy of containment when they didn't have any troops encircling Iraq and they weren't spending their taxpayers' money on preventing Saddam from rebuilding his military capabilities and acquiring the means to produce weapons of mass destruction.

Friends can disagree and disappointment shouldn't be allowed to fester until it becomes something more serious and damaging for a relationship. As the war continued and our forces moved steadily toward Baghdad, I took every opportunity to say that the fundamentals of Canada–US relations were too solid and the goodwill between our nations too great for our disagreement over Iraq to have long-term negative consequences. My government was grateful for Canada's support in Afghanistan and for the government's cooperation on a number of fronts in improving continental security. I welcomed statements by the prime minister and Foreign Minister John Manley that opened the door to the possibility of Canada playing a reconstruction role in post-war Iraq. And I thought it was important that the issue of Iraq not be allowed to overshadow the other matters that our governments needed to work on. Energy was one of the issues I continued to talk about in speeches and interviews, even while the troops were still advancing on Baghdad.

Just when I thought the temperature was cooling down and our disagreement over Iraq was being managed, I was hit with news that sent it shooting up again. Commodore Roger Girouard, the Canadian in command of the nine-nation naval task force in the Persian Gulf, admitted to reporters that he had been ordered by

Ottawa not to hand over to the US–British coalition any captured Iraqis. This would have included even Saddam Hussein, his two sons, and members of Saddam's inner circle. When I heard this I was stunned. The Canadian government's explanation didn't help matters. The ships were in the gulf to hunt al Qaeda terrorists and escort US supply ships en route to Iraq. The Canadian commander was authorized to turn over suspected al Qaeda terrorists to US forces, but not terrorists or members of Saddam's regime fleeing Iraq. What was the commander supposed to do with captured Iraqis? According to Defence Minister John McCallum, they should be "turned over to an international court and brought to justice." The prospect of Saddam Hussein being intercepted by a Canadian ship in the gulf and then turned over to the International Criminal Court left me flabbergasted. At a private dinner hosted by the Insurance Bureau of Canada, I said flat out that the Canadian government's position was incomprehensible. This wasn't a remark intended for broader public consumption. But when it was reported by Alliance MP Jason Kenney, who was one of several politicians there, I had no intention of backing down.

All of this was happening just weeks before President Bush was scheduled to visit Ottawa on May 5, 2003. I had been asked several times, even before the war in Iraq began, whether the president's visit might be cancelled because of the Canadian government's position on the war and what some saw as the prime minister's unwillingness to take seriously the spate of anti-American comments from people in his own party. Official visits can be cancelled and postponed for all sorts of reasons and we were, after all, at war. In the end, it was an accumulation of things that led to the postponement of President Bush's visit. The White House was already unhappy enough with the Canadian government's sniping about the war being unjustified, its insistence that multilateralism and the UN were the only legitimate channels for dealing with Iraq or any outlaw regime, and the personal attacks directed at the president. Everyone sensed that the visit had been in jeopardy for a while. The matter of the Canadian government not being willing to turn over fugitive Iraqis was the final straw.

There is no doubt that the visit would have gone ahead as planned if Canada had joined the coalition in Iraq. It might even have gone ahead if the government had delivered on its assurances that when the war began it would refrain from criticizing my government. But that's not what happened. Instead, the Canadian government sent out a string of mixed messages and every time I thought we had taken a step forward, something pushed us two steps back. A visit to talk about rebuilding Iraq with a coalition member would have been more likely to happen. And in the end that's what transpired. Australia's Prime Minister John Howard visited the president at his ranch in Crawford on the day George Bush was supposed to have met with Jean Chrétien. The president's thinking was that you first need to talk to the people fighting the war with you. That's the first order of business. So the cancellation of the visit, when it was finally announced, came as no great surprise.

There's not much doubt that the weeks leading up to and after the invasion of Iraq were stressful times in Canada–US relations. My decision to be forthright and plainspoken in explaining my government's feelings to the Canadian people was applauded by many and condemned by some. That's what happens when you engage in public diplomacy. I thought it was the right way to proceed then, and as I look back on those turbulent weeks I still think it was the right thing to do. It would have been wrong to let Canadians think that my government was just fine with Ottawa's decision on the war. It wasn't fine, and people needed to hear this. Quiet diplomacy was not what the situation called for. I wouldn't have been doing my job as the person representing my country's interests in Canada, and Canadians might have had the mistaken impression that their government's refusal to support us was viewed as insignificant in Washington.

When I think back on the argument about whether Canada should have joined the Iraq invasion, I like to recall a letter to a newspaper that appeared just after Prime Minister Chrétien announced that Canada would not participate. It was written by George Petrolekas, who was an officer with the Canadian Forces peacekeeping mission in Bosnia in 1993–94. He is a man who served his country and the cause of world peace in a dangerous place at a perilous time. He is someone who knows the importance of being there for a friend and ally. Here is one of his memories:

> In 1993, one cold, blustery and grey afternoon in Bosnia,
> Canadian soldiers wearing blue UN berets received an ulti-
> matum from one of the warring factions to leave positions
> that kept humanitarian aid flowing within the hour or die.
> So, like good Canadian peacekeepers, we went to negotiate,
> speaking softly but unfortunately lacking a big stick. In a
> flash of imagination, we called the Americans who were
> enforcing a no-fly zone over Bosnia. Their airplanes were
> not equipped for low-level attack, though that did not
> deter them.
>
> My Commanding Officer, David Moore, was standing
> on that bridge facing down the faction which threatened us
> all as American fighters sped to our position to firm up our
> resolve with something approximating a big stick. They
> swooped in low and fast, their sonic booms reverberating off

the valley walls. The other side blinked and the death threat was removed. "Ah, the sound of freedom," my CO said.

George Petrolekas was one of many Canadians I met who were genuinely concerned about Canada and its relationship to the United States. I am grateful that he took the time to write that letter. After my disappointments of the previous weeks it was a helpful reminder that at least some Canadians understood the kind of support that is expected within a family.

CHAPTER EIGHT

Perplexed

The august portrait of John George Diefenbaker, Canada's thirteenth prime minister, hangs in the Centre Block of the Parliament Buildings in Ottawa, and there he scowls at the passing world. Diefenbaker was a strong Canadian nationalist and a great orator whose populist rhetoric would have moved the people of the American Midwest as it did his fellow citizens in Saskatchewan. But in my final weeks as United States ambassador to Canada, there were other reasons to think about John George Diefenbaker. He made history in many ways during his six years as prime minister, but he may be best remembered for the decision that was critical in the downfall of his own government in 1963. I read accounts that said Diefenbaker, already beset by a host of other problems, reneged on his promise to accept warheads for the American Bomarc missiles that were on Canadian territory as part of Canada's participation in NORAD. In the resultant uproar, the Diefenbaker government fell. Diefenbaker's Conservatives were succeeded by the Liberal government of Lester B. Pearson, who accepted warheads for the Bomarc missiles on Canadian soil, although the decision caused considerable consternation within the ranks of his party.

The scowling portrait of John Diefenbaker is a colorful reminder that missiles have been a recurring source of conflict between Canada and the United States. The Bomarc crisis was shaking relations between the two countries four decades before I arrived in Ottawa. Pierre Trudeau's Liberal government had a missile problem, if not a missile crisis, as did Brian Mulroney's Conservatives. So it is a long and contentious history, and I knew from my first days on the job that missiles would again be a problem. As in the past, the bone of contention is Canadian sovereignty and the government's concern that sovereignty would be compromised if Canada participated in the US missile defense system. As someone told me, missiles are a kind of "third rail" issue in Canadian–American relations. Sad but true.

Even before I got to Ottawa, I knew that selling the idea of missile defense would be a challenge. But my government very much wanted the cooperation of the Canadian government and its participation in the missile defense system. But I did believe that the arguments in favor of Canada's cooperation were so strong and our history of cooperation in missile defense so long and successful, that Canada's government would be ultimately willing to sign on.

I was wrong. Four years after my arrival in Ottawa, despite all my early certainty about the obvious logic of the missile defense system, I was astounded by Prime Minister Paul Martin's announcement on February 24, 2005, that Canada would not take part. It just didn't make sense to me. Half a year earlier, just after the re-election of the Liberal government, I felt confident that our countries would be partners in this important enterprise. I knew that the government's minority status in Parliament complicated the picture somewhat, but my expectation was that Prime Minister Martin and his government shared our view and were willing to face down the critics of Canadian participation in missile defense. How wrong I was.

Looking back, what is so strange about the missile defense debate is that the two sides seemed to be looking at quite different problems. The Canadians seemed to believe that they could bottle up Canada and its vulnerability quite apart from the rest of the continent. But the reality is a shared geography in which the border is a line on a map that can't be seen from a missile launched from abroad. A missile targeted at Chicago, Seattle, Detroit or New York might well inadvertently hit Canada. It could even be targeted at Canada. Or, depending on its launch site, it could pass over Canadian airspace on its route to an American target. A missile destined for the US is not going to vary its route so that it does not travel through or over Canadian airspace. Nor do the niceties of whose airspace is where figure in a US response. Whatever the target, a US decision to intercept a missile would probably be made well before it was over American airspace.

Then there is the reality of a common threat. Al Qaeda has said that it makes no distinction between support for the United States in Afghanistan, where Canada played an active combat role, and Iraq, where Canada was not a member of the US-led coalition. Therefore Canada is a potential terrorist target.

During my four years as ambassador, I must have given dozens of speeches, in which I talked about the network of treaties and institutions that our two countries have developed over three generations—treaties and institutions that give Canada a seat at the table and respect Canadian sovereignty. As a start on shared continental defense, I could point to the 1940 creation of the Permanent Joint Board of Defense. And from there we can move right up to the summer of 2004 when the Canadian government accepted changes to the NORAD agreement. At the time, I thought those changes signaled its determination to stay a full partner in continental defense. These amendments were a critical aspect of the missile defense system, basing its integrated tactical warning and attack assessment at NORAD. But because of the Canadian government's decision not to participate in the actual missile defense system, Canadian soldiers now will work to detect a missile launch and its track, but then they will be required to leave the room when a decision has to be made about whether to intercept it — even if the missile's target is Canada! It made no sense then and it makes no sense now.

As the events of September 11 demonstrated, global terrorism has profoundly transformed the threats that governments must be prepared to encounter and stop. In my country, there has been a bipartisan consensus on the need for a missile defense shield since the late-1980s. Under four presidents, almost $50 billion has been invested in developing the system. At their 2002 meeting in Prague, NATO members agreed to "examine options for protecting alliance territory, forces and population centers against the full range of missile threats." Britain, Australia and Japan are already active partners with the United States in developing a ballistic missile defense system. Denmark is participating by agreeing to upgrades of the US radar system in Greenland. Even Russia has shown interest. How Canada, our next-door neighbor with whom we effectively share airspace and to whom we are joined by ties more intimate than those between any other two countries, could remain on the sideline was beyond my comprehension.

As I saw it, missile defense was part of the same package that included more Canadian military spending and a willingness to help in the war on terror. That was the package of measures that had to be undertaken to protect national security in the world after September

11. I thought Paul Martin put it well during his campaign for the Liberal Party leadership when he said, "September 11 has essentially changed the game fundamentally.... What we should increase defence spending upon is the model that's arisen out of September 11, which is essentially the fight against terrorism." And as prime minister I believe he has lived up to his word. Prime Minister Martin's 2005 budget earmarked about $13 billion over five years for new military spending.

I took real satisfaction that the debate on Canadian military spending shifted significantly during my four years as ambassador. The new consensus that had emerged was that Canada needed to reinvest in its military, after years of flirtation with the soft power notion that you can wield influence abroad without being able to put boots on the ground and planes in the air. I don't by any means take sole credit for this change. David Pratt, John Manley, Major-General (retired) Lewis MacKenzie and many others made the same arguments and kept the issue prominent. But I also noticed that whenever I gave a speech or interview on Canadian defense spending and policy, headlines followed. That's the way public diplomacy works.

As for Canada as an ally in the war on terror, I have nothing but praise for the Canadian government, the Canadian Forces and Canada's intelligence and law enforcement agencies. Of course my government was disappointed when Prime Minister Chrétien's government decided not to join the coalition in Iraq. And I meant every word that I said in my Toronto speech, just after the government's announcement, when I expressed my feeling that we had been let down by family. Those words were from the heart.

It would have been another significant milestone in our friendship to have Canada on board in Iraq. But looking at the total picture of the war against terror, Canada supports the US very well. Shoulder to shoulder in Afghanistan. Cooperating in the development and implementation of intelligence gathering and more common immigration measuring under the Smart Border Action Plan. Helping to cripple the finances and support network of terrorist groups like Hezbollah, Hamas, Islamic Jihad and, of course, al Qaeda. The fact that the Canadian government did not commit to the liberation of Iraq was a major disappointment. I never felt, though, that it detracted in any major way from Canada's resolve to combat the sources of global terrorism.

But when it comes to missile defense, I was more than puzzled that the Canadian government finally, after years of vacillation, said no to joining with us in a continental system. I was perplexed by a decision that just made no sense to me. The arguments against Canadian participation seemed to me so ill-informed and wrong-headed that I had a hard time understanding how anyone could take them seriously. Except that, in the end, I understood that politics had carried the day over common sense and, I believe, over Canada's national self-interest.

It was not an outcome that I would have predicted two years earlier. When I met the Canadian Senate foreign affairs committee in April of 2003, I felt upbeat about the prospects of Canada joining with us in missile defense. Cabinet was discussing the issue and several in Prime Minister Chrétien's government, including Defence Minister John McCallum, Deputy Prime Minister John Manley and Foreign Affairs Minister Bill Graham had all spoken publicly in favor of cooperating with the United States on missile defense. Canadian military and foreign affairs officials had been to NORAD headquarters in Colorado Springs and had seen simulations of the missile defense system. They brought back positive reports. And Canadian public opinion, while divided on the issue, certainly was not strongly opposed to Canadian participation except in the province of Quebec. I thought, and I still believe, that all that was necessary was for the Canadian government to exercise leadership on this issue.

Instead, there was vacillation and delay. I understood that missile defense had long been a contentious issue in Canadian politics. That portrait of John Diefenbaker was always there to remind me of just how contentious and even politically lethal it could be for Canadian politicians. But I expected that even if Prime Minister Chrétien wouldn't support missile defense, his successor would. Paul Martin was the odds-on favorite to win the leadership of the Liberal Party and succeed Chrétien as prime minister. I liked what I heard from Martin on this issue. It was clear and it made sense. "It's conceivable that a missile could be going over Canadian airspace," he said in an April 2003 interview. "And you know what? If a missile is going over Canadian airspace, I want to know. I want to be at the table before that happens."

Critics of missile defense would always trot out arguments about Canadian sovereignty being compromised by cooperation with the United States. This was a theme that hadn't changed since Diefenbaker's time. But Paul Martin had an answer, and I thought it was the right answer: "You want to talk about sovereignty? My sovereignty says you don't send missiles up over my airspace unless I'm there."

Something obviously happened between April 2003, when leadership candidate Paul Martin made those comments and when the prospects for Canadian participation in a continental missile defense plan looked promising, and Prime Minister Martin's decision in February 2005 to say no to missile defense. During those nearly two years of indecision and mixed signals there were clearly warning signs. Yet at no point did I believe that the roadblocks, hesitations and opposition would be enough to produce such a disappointing outcome.

One of the first warning signs was a vote in the House of Commons in June 2003. The Canadian Alliance, later to become the Conservative Party, tabled a motion in favor of having NORAD take responsibility for command of a continental missile defense system. This non-binding resolution was approved by a vote of 156 to 73. That was the good news. The bad news was that 38 Liberal MPs voted against the motion. Most of those Liberals were from Quebec. The other bad news—although how bad was not obvious to me at the time—was that Paul Martin skipped the vote, saying that he found the Alliance motion to be "ambiguous" because it might permit the weaponization of space. I understood that this was a delicate issue and that Martin was in the thick of a leadership race, so I didn't attribute much importance to his unwillingness to support the motion.

The fact that almost all Quebec's MPs, both Liberal and Bloc Quebecois, voted against the motion was a more serious matter. I had spoken with the recently elected premier of Quebec, Jean Charest, during a visit to Quebec City in late April 2003. The conversation turned to the issue of missile defense and Charest told me point-blank that a Liberal government would never agree to participate in such a plan before the federal election. If it did, he said, the Liberals would be handing a major political gift to the Bloc Quebecois. Quebeckers didn't like the idea of missile defense. They hadn't supported the Gulf War in 1991 and they were overwhelmingly opposed to the war in Iraq. More than other Canadians, he said, Quebeckers tended to believe that national security could best be protected by the soft power repertoire of international institutions and law and multilateral diplomacy, and that it was actually threatened by robust military preparedness.

I told Premier Charest that I understood and respected the views of Quebeckers. I knew that Quebec was otherwise very pro-American and very supportive of free trade. I also knew that there was a history of strong anti-war sentiment in Quebec and that this had been a part of the distinctive Quebec culture for a long time. Charest agreed with me that the strong opposition among Quebeckers to the war in Iraq should not be interpreted as anti-Americanism.

At the same time I believed that the right leadership could bring some people around to seeing that missile defense made sense for Canada. I knew what had happened to John Diefenbaker, but I also knew about Pierre Trudeau, who had wrestled with the issue of missile defense in the 1980s and won. Cruise missiles were an important part of the military arsenal of the United States and NATO, but the idea of testing them on Canadian soil inspired loud and bitter opposition. Demonstrations on Parliament Hill and even a court challenge to Ottawa's authority to allow these tests might have broken the resolve of some leaders. As the vacillation on missile defense continued under Prime Minister Chrétien and then Prime Minister Martin, I wondered how it was that Trudeau, well known for his reservations about the military and his unflinching defense of Canadian sovereignty, was willing to stare down the opposition to cruise missile testing. Trudeau accepted that Canada had obligations under NATO and NORAD, yet his successors seemed unwilling to show the same sort of leadership.

It certainly wasn't as if there was not considerable support in Parliament for Canadian participation in continental missile defense. Consider the vote of 156 to 73. The Alliance motion had passed by a better than 2 to 1 ratio. It seemed to me that, politically, there was a lot there for any prime minister to work with.

Once Paul Martin was sworn in as prime minister and we started to talk about a date for him to meet with President Bush, I was confident that we would be able to get the missile defense plan back on track. Prime Minister Martin's choice for the defense portfolio, David Pratt, was someone who I'd gotten to know well over the previous three years. Pratt had been the chair of the House of Commons defence committee and was one of the strongest advocates in the Liberal Party of increased defense spending. I know that he was personally disappointed at his government's decision not to join in the coalition in Iraq. We had talked many times and I knew that he was a dependable advocate of Canadian missile defense and well versed on security issues. With Pratt steering the issue through cabinet I felt confident about the likelihood of Canada signing on. At the same time I understood that there were some real limits on just how far the Canadian government was likely to go on continental missile defense. Government officials had been saying that Canada was not likely to make a financial contribution to missile defense or permit interceptor rocket launchers to be based on Canadian territory. Pratt told me that the door was not closed to these possibilities, but I knew that a politically realistic scenario might be the use of Canadian territory for radar sites only. We already had agreements for radar facilities with the UK and Danish governments and were then negotiating with Denmark to upgrade our early warning radar facilities in Greenland for a missile defence mission, which was subsequently agreed to in mid-2004.

Despite the occasional eruptions of opposition I was encouraged by the widespread consensus that seemed to be developing among Canadian opinion-leaders that continental missile defense had become a matter of "when" and no longer of "if." "Political Ottawa is beginning to accept what military Ottawa has known for a long time," said David Bercuson, one of Canada's most respected historians, "there will be missile defense." But time was becoming a factor. My government planned to begin the first stage of a missile defense system in

October 2004, with interceptor sites in Alaska and California. For obvious reasons we very much wanted Canada to participate. I saw, however, that the politics of this issue in Canada were getting more complicated. In late February 2004, the Bloc Quebecois tabled a motion in the House of Commons calling for Ottawa to break off talks with my government on missile defense only a month after these talks had begun. It was defeated by a wide margin, 155 to 71. But I was concerned that 29 Liberals, most of them from Quebec, had voted for the BQ motion. And several Liberals who voted against the motion took pains to say that they were not necessarily supportive of missile defense but were taking a wait-and-see attitude toward the negotiations.

The complicating factor now, of course, was the election that everyone expected to be called sooner rather than later. As a longtime politician I appreciated the fact that you never want to hand your opponent an issue that he or she can use against you. So Prime Minister Martin's reluctance to commit himself one way or the other struck me as simple prudence. This was particularly so after his party's polling numbers in Quebec dropped significantly as a result of allegations of fraud and corruption in the distribution of government advertising monies in Quebec—the political mess that became known as the sponsorship scandal. The prospect of a Liberal minority government, unthinkable only weeks before, suddenly became a real possibility. I knew that the prime minister would have enough to deal with in fighting back the challenge of a resurgent BQ without having to justify continental missile defense to voters. So when President Bush and Prime Minister Martin met in Washington, the issue was not even on the official agenda.

Inevitably, though, it came up in the conversation. And naturally enough the Canadian reporters asked the prime minister about missile defense at the press conference that followed. "We will reach a decision in due course," was the message Prime Minister Martin gave to the president. He also repeated Canada's concern that continental missile defense should not result in the weaponization of space. All this, I thought, was fair enough—but once the election was over and the dust had settled, a decision would need to be reached.

The evening of the 2004 Canadian election I was at the Residence watching the returns with Bob Durand, who had been my secretary of environmental affairs when I was governor of Massachusetts, and Chuck Anastas, Bob's business partner. Like me, both Bob and Chuck were from Hudson; although they were both Democrats, we had worked together on a number of state campaigns over the years. I remember that when Jack Layton came out to talk to his supporters, after it had become clear that the NDP had not done as well as he had hoped, Bob and Chuck turned to me and asked, "Is he going to be the next PM?" Layton might have sounded like he had won that night, but I explained that he was in fact the leader of a small left-wing party that was in last place in the House of Commons.

Watching the returns that evening, I saw that David Pratt was in trouble in his riding of Nepean-Carleton. I had come to know Pratt and I appreciated his strong support for missile defense during the several months when he was minister of defense. He ended up losing his seat in the House of Commons. I called him the next day and expressed my regrets. I suppose some of his caucus and even cabinet colleagues might have thought Pratt too pro-American, but in fact he was someone who understood what was truly in Canada's national interest and who refused to be hoodwinked by inaccurate arguments about sovereignty and the so-called weaponization of space.

With the defeat of Pratt, we had lost a solid ally in cabinet, but even more troubling was the overall election outcome. The Bloc had increased their strength in Quebec and the NDP almost doubled its number of seats in the House. The new Conservative Party also made gains, but the Conservatives had faltered badly in the final days of the nasty campaign. So Martin's Liberals remained on top but they had been reduced to a minority government. That obviously did not bode well for negotiations on missile defense, but at the same time I believed that the momentum we had developed and the support that we had in cabinet were enough to win the day. It would take leadership from the prime minister, but that's what leaders are elected to do. Everyone knew the clock was ticking. My government wanted to start deployment of the missile system in a matter of months. The day after the elections, I stated publicly that my government understood that the minority government situation would present some challenges, but that we hoped Ottawa would make a favorable decision on missile defense.

The next month at the Calgary Stampede, I advocated for missile defense again. Defense experts and opposition critics had been saying from the beginning of the debate on missile defense that failure by Canada to participate could bring about the demise of NORAD. I didn't go that far, but I said that NORAD could suffer if Canada chose not to join in missile defense. That wasn't just my assessment. Canadian Lieutenant-General Rick Findley, NORAD's deputy commander, echoed my view. "We already do missile warning," he said, "Why wouldn't you want to be part of the last chunk?"

In the middle of the summer, the Canadian and American governments reached an agreement on NORAD, which I thought moved everything another step toward a decision on missile defense. The agreement was amended to extend NORAD's aerospace warning and detection to include missile defense. In welcoming the amendment, I took pains to emphasize that it did not in any way change the missions performed by Canadian personnel assigned to NORAD.

And I added that we looked forward to continuing discussions with the Canadian government on its full participation in a continental missile defense system.

Slowly, very slowly, the pieces of an agreement on missile defense seemed to be coming together. We knew that the Canadian government did not want to spend any money on missile defense. The US accepts that responsibility. Also, the Canadian government wanted an exit mechanism to be part of any agreement, so that if it decided Canadian participation was no longer in the nation's interest it could withdraw from the missile defense system. The US explained to Canada that the US Missile Defense Agency was conducting a space-based interceptor research and development program. Furthermore, Canada was told that if the threat to the US evolves in the future further increasing the danger to our population and territory, and space-based interceptor systems are technologically ready for deployment, the US president would have that option to excerise. If the president decided to deploy space-based interceptors, Ottawa could end its participation in the US missile defense system and program as its sovereign right.

President Bush was scheduled to make his first state visit to Canada at the end of November. I had hoped that negotiations would have reached a point where we could announce a deal on Canadian participation in continental missile defense. To my great disappointment, we couldn't even get the issue onto the formal agenda for the talks between the president and the prime minister. Two years of off-and-on negotiations and we still had to keep up the pretence that this was not a vitally important issue between us.

Of course, the issue came up anyway during the talks in Ottawa. President Bush raised it because he couldn't understand what the basis was for the Canadian government's reluctance to sign on to missile defense, particularly after the amendment to NORAD the previous summer. Like me, the president saw it as being in Canada's sovereign and national interests to participate in determining what would happen to an incoming missile flying a trajectory over Canadian territory. Prime Minister Martin explained to the president the problem of a minority government and the fact that he was formally committed to holding a vote in the House of Commons on any missile defense agreement. Well, there had already been two votes on motions tabled by the Alliance and the Bloc and those opposed to missile defense had been pretty solidly thumped on both occasions. We could all do the arithmetic. Even if all the BQ and NDP members voted against missile defense, joined by 30 or even 40 Liberals, a third vote on missile defense would still pass if all the Conservatives voted for it. It might be divisive and the debate acrimonious, but I believed it would have been supported by a majority of Liberals and virtually all of the Conservative members of the House.

After their private talks, when the two leaders emerged for a photo session and to make their statements to the press, President Bush decided that it was time for him to do a bit of public diplomacy. He started by thanking the Canadian government and the Canadian people for their warm reception, "especially the Canadian people who came out to wave—with all five fingers." When the president turned to the substance of his talks with Prime Minister Martin, some people were visibly surprised: "We talked about the future of NORAD and how that organization can best meet emerging threats and safeguard our continent against attack from ballistic missiles." The president made it clear that he hoped the Canadian government would sign on as a partner in missile defense, echoing the public remarks that I had been making for quite some time. Martin was obviously not at ease having to respond to the president's unmistakably blunt words. But frankly, we were approaching the point where inde-cision on this issue was becoming paralysis. Something needed to be done to break the log-jam.

We held numerous rounds of consultations with the Canadian government about its participation in continental missile defense. We had the vast majority of respected Canadian defense experts in our corner. And we'd been talking about the issue for the better part of four years. Despite all of that, I sensed that the momentum and optimism that had existed even a few months earlier had dissipated. In fact, almost every statement from the Canadian government seemed to indicate that we were as far from an agreement as ever. Prime Minister Martin continued to say that Canada would make a decision when it was in Canada's interests to do so. When that day would ever arrive was not clear.

Even as all of this was happening and my frustration with a process that seemed to be stalled was mounting, the friendship that Jan and I had developed with Prime Minister and Sheila Martin remained unshaken. This is one of the lessons that I've learned from over 30 years in public life. Don't let policy differences poison per-sonal relations. A few days into the new year, the Prime Minister's Office called just as I got home and asked whether we could join the Martins for dinner. Dress would be casual. An hour later, Prime Minister Martin rang the doorbell at the Residence and then the four of us were on our way to the Urban Pear in the Glebe. We had a won-derful evening together. We shared family stories and updated the Martins on our travels across Canada. Even the occasional mention of missile defense didn't spoil our private friendship.

Finally, a decision was announced. It was not the decision that I had hoped would be reached. But I can't say that I was surprised in the end. The Canadian government announced that it would not join with us in continental missile defense. Although I was not surprised, I was perplexed. I just didn't get it. It seemed to me quite obvious that it was in Canada's sovereign interest to be at the table when decisions were made about the defense of North America, decisions with implications for Canadian territory. Paul Martin had believed this too, I recalled, before becoming prime minister. I made clear what the Canadian government already knew, that the United States was determined to deploy a missile defense system and that this could well result in scenarios where missiles passing through Canadian airspace would be intercepted by rockets fired from the United States or from sea-based launchers. And unlike the arrangement under NORAD, no Canadian would be part of the decision-making process. As a result of the Canadian government's decision to say no to missile defense, we now had the potential for the extraordinary and totally illogical scenario of Canadian and American soldiers working together on missile detection and tracking, but even if a missile was headed to Canada, the Canadian soldiers at NORAD would have to leave the room when the decision about interception had to be made. This just made no sense whatsoever. Was that what Canadians wanted? Is that what the defense of Canadian sovereignty meant? Putting decisions about Canada's sovereignty in the hands of another country?

To better explain this, let's imagine that the unlikely happens and an incoming missile is way off target and is heading for Canada's North. Canada will be out of the protocols at NORAD. And with a decision that must be made very quickly—within minutes—Canada will be totally out of the loop. Canada will thus cede a sovereign decision to the United States. The US may have different sovereign interests at stake from those of Canada. For example, the cost of taking out the missile. Canada's sovereign interest could be protecting valuable natural resources and possibly people in that barren part of the country. It amounts to an amazing giveaway of sovereignty.

I'm convinced that there was indecision at the highest levels right to the end. Frank McKenna, Canada's newly appointed ambassador to Washington, had testified before the Commons foreign affairs committee just days before, saying that Canada had all but joined the missile defense system as a result of the amendment to the NORAD agreement the previous summer. I thought so too, when that amendment was agreed to, but the weeks after the president's December visit to Ottawa had left me feeling much less confident about the outcome. I had heard rumors that the government had reached a negative decision the week before the formal announcement. If McKenna heard these rumors too, then I guess he simply couldn't believe them.

What added to the disappointment of the decision was the clumsy manner in which it was announced. Foreign Affairs Minister Pierre Pettigrew communicated the decision to Secretary of State Condi Rice at the NATO summit in Brussels. The timing and method of the announcement certainly were not well received in Washington. Just when the president was in Europe trying to show some unity with NATO allies after the rift that had opened over Iraq, our close ally and next-door neighbor chose that moment to signal its rejection of something that we considered to be crucial to our future security. Then there was the fact that the prime minister did not tell the president himself, although the two men were both at the NATO meeting and at several points were standing side by side. But not a word was said. All in all, it was an inept ending to a frustrating process.

Long before the Canadian government announced its decision on February 24, I had spent many hours thinking through the government's obvious hesitation to sign on, and about the ferocity of some of the criticisms of Canadian participation in missile defense. I understood very well that the Liberal Party had within its ranks pockets of strong opposition, particularly from its women's and Quebec wings. And I understood the delicate task of holding on to power in the minority government in which Prime Minister Martin found himself. Even if the government had the numbers to win a vote on missile defense in the House, such a victory might be at the price of needed support from NDP or BQ members on some other vote that could bring down the government. And I also understood that signing on for missile defense would make matters difficult for many Liberal candidates in the next election campaign, whenever that might be. But, despite all of this, I was convinced that with leadership from the prime minister, making the case that participation in missile defense was in Canada's security *and* sovereignty interests, virtually all of the Conservatives would have been with him, and all but a relatively small number of Liberal MPs.

In defense of Prime Minister Martin, he was not the only one whose leadership might have been judged wavering on this issue. The Conservative Party was not exactly a model of clarity and principle during all of this. President Bush spoke with Conservative leader Stephen Harper during his 2004 trip to Ottawa and received a rather positive indication from him about where the Conservative Party would stand on this issue. But shortly before the government's rejection of missile defense was announced, Prime Minister Martin said that he was thinking of putting troops into Iraq to help train Iraqi security forces. The very first person to raise objections was Stephen Harper. The prime minister ended up beating a hasty retreat and said that the Canadian military trainers would only do their job outside of Iraq. Was this the same party that took every opportunity to castigate the government for not being supportive of its American ally? Once again, politics took precedence over policy.

But I also felt that there was more to this picture. In the final analysis I believe that much of the opposition to Canadian participation in missile defense was not based on the actual proposal at all. After all, we weren't asking Canada to contribute money or allow interceptor rockets on its soil. And we were not intending to "weaponize" space, despite NDP leader Jack Layton's claims that both the president and Colin Powell admitted to him that this was the plan. I don't say that Mr. Layton was lying when he made this claim, but I think that either his hearing was off or he simply hears what he wants to hear. Finally, no one can seriously believe that Canadian sovereignty is better protected by permitting others to make unilateral decisions that could have implications for Canadian territory.

In the end, the government capitulated to a minority of its own MPs who, I believe, were uneasy about anything that might be construed as expanding military cooperation with the United States. In the case of some, this uneasiness was accompanied by a virulent dislike of President Bush and a belief that any policy he supported must be bad for Canada and the world. Our countries have long been the best of friends, but I know that alongside this friendship there has also existed an uneasiness among many Canadians about their much larger neighbor and a belief that to get too close would somehow be damaging for Canadian interests and independence. Apparently that is what Prime Minister Diefenbaker believed back in 1963, when he went back on his promise to fulfill Canada's NORAD obligations. Whether he was right or wrong I leave to Canadian historians to judge. But I'm sure that the missile defense decision made by the Canadian government in 2005 is not one that historians will judge to have been in the best interests of Canadian security and sovereignty.

CHAPTER NINE

At Home in Ottawa

When Jan and I moved into the Residence, we faced a daunting task. It was a wonderful building, all 32 rooms, with beautiful grounds and breathtaking views. But when all the redecorating had been finished and all the asbestos had been removed, we wanted to put our personal mark on the place. For the next four years, it was not going to be just the Residence of the Ambassador of the United States. It was going to be our home, and as much as possible we wanted it to feel that way to ourselves and to others.

We decided the way to put our stamp on the Residence was through art and books. The books were those we brought from home in Massachusetts and those we acquired in Canada after our arrival; most of the art came as a result of the Art in Embassies program that is run by the State Department.

In the spacious formal entrance to the Residence was a painting of Boston Harbor at the turn of the nineteenth century, which was the kind of thing you might expect from a Massachusetts couple. That was one of my favorites, as was another that we hung directly opposite the front entrance: a large map of the city of Velletri, not far from Rome, where most of my Italian family lives. Family has always been the center of our lives, so giving pride of place to that treasured souvenir was a natural choice for us, and in the main salon we provided a touch of home with our favorite family photos of our daughters, Kate and Anne, and of Anne and Craig Adams on the day of their wedding, flanked by RCMP officers in their signature scarlet tunics.

I must confess that not everything was a personal favorite. In fact, some of what made its way onto the walls of the Residence left me puzzled. Jan and I have rather different tastes. She is modern and abstract, I am fairly traditional. I like nineteenth century landscapes of the Hudson River; as for Jan's choices, she used to joke that I was planning to have buttons made that would read, "I am not responsible for the art work."

One large photograph on which we both agreed was a favorite of a quite different order. It was a large black-and-white picture, about a meter wide, of a motorcade and a large crowd, with the Massachusetts state house in the background. Someone is standing up in the limousine, visible above the open sun roof, waving to the crowds. Sometimes I would challenge guests to try to identify this "important person," as I would tell them. There were all sorts of guesses during our four years in Ottawa, most of them wrong. The important person in the photo was Pope John Paul II, taken on the occasion of his 1979 visit to the United States. It was his first visit to America as Pope. This was before his attempted assassination and the "pope-mobile" that he afterwards used when traveling through crowds.

As a member of the state legislature, I had been invited to watch the arrival ceremony of the Pope at Logan Airport. I brought along our two-year old daughter, Kate, while Jan and baby Anne watched the Pope's arrival on television at home. I remember the Pope descending the steps of a huge Air Lingus jet and kissing the ground on his arrival in the United States. Kate tells me that she remembers this too, despite her young age. My friend, photographer Lincoln Russell, took the picture of the motorcade and sent it to us after we had moved to Ottawa. It represented many things that were important to me.

Despite our different views of art, Jan and I did agree on one thing. Both of us wanted to feature the newest art that had been exhibited at the Massachusetts Museum of Contemporary Arts (Mass MoCA) in North Adams, once a textile mill town in the western part of the state. For us, that museum had a particular personal significance. The mills closed years ago and North Adams went into decline. Jobs disappeared, stores closed, people left, and the future looked bleak. As governor of Massachusetts, I supported the transformation of the closed mill complex and a 13-acre site into the Mass MoCA, the world's largest center for contemporary arts. This was Lietenant Governor Jane Swift's home town, and she had been a passionate advocate for this project since her days in the state Senate. The historic mill complex has been converted into a series of "new art" exhibition and performance spaces. There are also state-of-the-art sculpture and new media studios, stages for the performing arts, a 700-seat theater, and more than 250,000 square feet of gallery space. Mass MoCA proved to be the engine for the revitalization of North Adams and the surrounding area, transforming this one-time industrial community into a post-industrial culture and tourism-based economy.

On the day of Mass MoCA's grand opening there were about 10,000 visitors. I remember gingerly moving through a barely shoulder-width maze of paths that were illuminated with a glaring, acid-green fluorescent light. My state police officers thought I would get stuck. This, I was told, was an example of installation art by Bruce Nauman. I was reassured to hear Mass MoCA's director, Joe Thompson, refer to it as "psychologically daunting." From the moment we got the word that we were headed for Ottawa, Jan and I knew that we wanted to display the work of some of Mass MoCA's artists in the Residence. Jan took the lead, working with Joe Thompson and the Art in Embassies curators at the State Department. With their guidance and coordination, we borrowed some of the most significant work from the Mass MoCA artists for the Residence in Ottawa. The Art in Embassies program was one of the earliest public diplomacy initiatives, conceived back in 1964 as a way of conveying American culture abroad. When Jan and I learned about it at "ambassador school," we knew immediately that we wanted to use the opportunity to showcase some of Mass MoCA's artists.

One of the pieces that generated the most comment over the years, possibly became of its location just feet from the dining room table, is actually brocade drapery. It's called "A Permutational Unfolding," and was created by New York sculptor and installation artist Eve Andrée Laramée. The intricate images in this lush drapery explore the history of digital technology, incorporating pictures of Joseph-Marie Jacquard, who in 1801 invented a loom that operated on a binary system of punched cards, and Ada Lovelace, Lord Byron's daughter and an important patron of scientists and mathematicians in the nineteenth century. There are circuit boards, punch cards and various early automated devices throughout the work. Had chef's creations not been so exceptional, dinner guests might have had a hard time pulling their attention away from this mesmerizing piece of art.

Jan has an unquenchable passion for books. I think she looked on the fact that the official residence had 32 rooms as a challenge to fill all the available coffee and end tables and the shelves with books of all sorts. I made my contributions too, but Jan is the hardcore bibliophile in the family. Guests at the Residence would invariably pick up a book that caught their eye and always seemed to be surprised that we had enough tomes to start a respectable bookstore.

Actually, I think a good bookstore would be hard pressed to carry the range of subjects covered in the personal library that we acquired while in Canada. Most of the sports books were my choices, including the *Boston Globe*'s beautiful book of photos commemorating the 2004 World Series victory of my Red Sox. (That was a sweet and long-awaited moment for every Boston fan.) Jan's tastes are a bit more eclectic than mine, and between us we almost covered the literary waterfront: *Our Life with the Rocket*; *The Meaning of the Dead Sea Scrolls*; *The Divine Ryans*; *The Story of Labrador*; *Chrétien*, Vol. 1; *No Holds Barred: My Life in Politics*; *Iqaluit*; *Elle: A Novel*; *1917 Halifax Explosion and American Response*; *First Nations Longhouse*; *Secret Ottawa*; *Paul Martin: In the Balance*. When Jan and I sat down to design the interior details of the townhouse that we had built for our return to Hudson, bookshelves—lots and lots of bookshelves—were at the top of Jan's priority list. My top priority was a high-definition television set to watch the Red Sox, the Patriots and my son-in-law's hockey games. Between the books and the photos, the art from the museum that Jan and I had supported when I was governor, and, of course, the old friends that we hosted and the new friends that we made while in Ottawa, the residence very quickly felt like home.

But it was mainly the people that we got to know while in Ottawa who really made us feel that we were at home. And at the top of the list was the staff of the official residence. Before coming to Ottawa we had never had an official residence. Massachusetts is one of only five states in the United States that does not provide its governor with an official residence. So living in an official mansion was new to us. We were used to doing everything from buying the groceries to cutting the grass. I even liked cutting the grass, although I have to admit that cutting the several acres of lawn on the Residence grounds would have eaten into my time in a way that doing the lawn in Hudson never did.

As it happened, we were fortunate to have a staff that deserved to be the envy of the Ottawa diplomatic community. Roger Beauregard was our residence manager *extraordinaire*. His job involved everything from greeting guests when they arrived to dealing with the most complicated and sensitive arrangements for dinners, receptions and meetings at the Residence. I saw immediately that this was someone whom I could trust and have confidence in to know what to do in all circumstances. When President and Mrs. Bush visited us at the end of November 2004, Roger was unfazed by the many security requirements. Whether it involved arrangements for a state dinner, overseeing the Fourth of July party for thousands of guests, or responding to a crisis situation, as happened on September 11, Roger was unflappable. Fluently bilingual, he was always ready to help Jan and I practice our French. What he thought of our progress I never asked, and he never said.

Lori Duval was our residence secretary and truly became Jan's right hand during four years of steady travel and entertaining. Jan would often accompany me on the hundreds of trips that I made across Canada and to official functions in the capital. But she would usually have her own itinerary, sometimes involving several events in a single day.

Scheduling busy itineraries and dealing with all the things, large and small, that can arise to knock them off course is no simple job. Lori and Jan received regular updates of my schedule and throughout the day Lori would receive information about changes to my plans and to the schedule of visits and activities at the Residence. Then in consultation with Karen Heide, my assistant, and Greta Poole, the embassy protocol office, Jan and Lori would sit down to determine when Jan should accompany me, when she could schedule her own events, or when she could just take time to read. Lori was one part scheduler par excellence and the other part counselor extraordinaire. No matter how hectic things got—and they often got very hectic—she remained a model of organization, good humor and sound advice.

Jan and I entertained thousands of guests at the Residence, from intimate dinner parties to big outdoor barbeques, and from black tie state affairs to blue jeans casual. A chef who can rise to all of these occasions, always hitting the right note and able to maintain his creative edge is a real prize. We had just such a chef in Dino Ovcaric. He was, it seemed to me, the embodiment of Canada in many ways. Born in Quebec of parents who had emigrated from Croatia, Dino was an artist in the kitchen, like a maestro who takes the music from notes on a page to an experience that people remember. It was always a pleasure sharing with him the compliments that his dinners elicited from guests.

Dino was assisted by Dana Gosso, the assistant executive chef. Dana's extensive culinary experience and easygoing manner formed a perfect complement to Dino's professional style. Gianni Bertazzo, the residence butler, brought old world charm to the household and made all of our guests feel welcome. Jovita (Nene) Ting and Estella Buenbiaje, maintained this large and busy home in wonderful condition, no matter how many visitors we had or how elaborate the function we hosted. And we always admired the meticulous work of the outdoor maintenance staff under the direction of Mike Lamothe; they took care of the official residence, the DCM's residence, the embassy grounds and the Marine house. We were lucky to work with such a talented and dedicated group of professionals.

The whole staff was used to the irregular hours, long days and unexpected circumstances that are all part of the job at an official residence as big and busy as the American one. Whenever possible, Jan and I would fend for ourselves on the weekends, letting the staff enjoy some well-deserved downtime. Jan would go out in the morning to buy several newspapers and I would make coffee and get breakfast ready. Sitting in the Residence's solarium, with its magnificent view on the Ottawa River, having breakfast and reading the weekend papers was a domestic pleasure we loved during our years in Canada. Quiet moments like these were rare.

"Ambassador school" had prepared Jan and me for the fact that the diplomatic life necessarily involves a good deal of socializing and entertaining. As the largest foreign mission in Ottawa, Jan and I were always being invited to far more functions than we could ever manager to attend. For diplomats with fewer staff and resources than the big missions have, these dinners and receptions can be important opportunities to acquire information and keep connected. This was never a problem for us. As much as we enjoyed the hospitality of other members of the diplomatic corps we always preferred to play host.

I knew that Canadians love hockey. As a longtime hockey fan who had spent many hours cheering the Bruins at the Boston Garden and my alma mater, the Boston College Eagles, I welcomed the prospect of living in a country where hockey is a sort of national religion. I don't think Jan had just my sports enthusiasms in mind when she said that Canada would be a great place to be ambassador, but for me it couldn't have worked out better.

When I was in the capital I never turned down an opportunity to go to an Ottawa Senators game at the Corel Centre. I particularly remember a time in March 2003 when the Bruins were in Ottawa to play the Senators. I had been to a game in Boston's Fleet Center the previous season and told Mike O'Connell, the Bruins general manager, that when the team came to play the Senators the next year that they were all invited to the Residence. Mike took me up on the offer. On a chilly March evening a year later, with a foot of snow on the ground, a Canada Coach bus pulled up in front of the Residence and the Boston Bruins with their coaches and managers came through the door.

We had a great time together. Several members of the Canadian government were there as well as Ottawa business people that we worked with, some members of the media, and former Bruins, including Hall of Famers Gerry Cheevers and Johnny Bucyk. We had also invited members of the diplomatic community from some of the players' home countries, including my friend Russian Ambassador Georgiy Mamedov. After I welcomed everyone, Marty Lapointe, the Bruins' right winger, presented me with a stadium seat from the old Boston Garden. It had my name inscribed on a plaque mounted on its base made of floorboards and the number "1" stenciled on the seat back. Jan said it was one of the best gifts I had ever received and I can't disagree. It occupied a place of honor in the television room of the Residence.

One of the fascinating things about an event like the one we had for the Bruins is the chemistry that takes place when you bring together people from different worlds. Here we had under the same roof hockey players, politicians, diplomats, business people and media types. But the main subject of conversation was hockey. This is one of the things that I like most about sport—its power to bring people together and kindle a shared passion. When the last guest took leave that evening, I still wasn't finished with hockey. I went upstairs to the television room where I had *Center Ice* on the satellite dish. There I watched my soon-to-be-son-in-law, Craig Adams, have the game of his career for the Carolina Hurricanes. Craig scored two goals and picked up an assist in a 6 to 5 win over the Columbus Blue jackets. A seat from the Garden and then a big game from my daughter's fiancé. It had been a perfect day.

Like so many other Canadian and American hockey fans, the cancellation of the 2004–2005 NHL season came as a huge disappointment to me. It was bad enough that there wouldn't be any professional hockey in the arenas and on television that year, but there was the added sting that my son-in-law would be sidelined by the bitter dispute between the players and the owners. Along with many of his NHL colleagues, Craig decided to go play in Europe until the impasse between the owners and the players was resolved. Although Jan and I were saddened by the thought that Anne and Craig would be so far away, Craig's choice of team helped take some of the edge off our sadness. He signed with the Milano Vipers, a decision that was based partly on the deep family connections that we had in Italy.

We attended two Vipers games, one against Bolzano and the second against Varese, when we visited Anne and Craig shortly before Christmas. Since Craig and the opposing team's goalie had been ejected from Milano's previous game against Bolzano—causing the Milano fans to riot—we arrived straight from the airport to find a row of armed *carabiniere* with riot shields standing guard in front of the fans in the lobby. Jan asked Anne what this police presence was all about, and she said simply, "Probably Craig." The Vipers fans were crazed, waving large flags and handmade signs, banging on drums and blowing horns throughout the game, smoking non-stop, and setting off fireworks in the stands. Craig told us after the game that he'd never seen a funnier sight from the ice than his American mother-in-law, the librarian, sitting amidst all this mayhem.

But as much as we enjoyed the atmosphere at the games—or at least I enjoyed the atmosphere—we were hoping that Anne and

Craig would soon be back home. We returned to Italy shortly after I departed my post as ambassador, this time with John and Agnieszka McDermott. We attended two Italian league playoff hockey games and spent Easter on the Isle of Capri with my cousins Ornella and Pietro Palieri, and Lamberto and Gloria Cellucci and their children Francesco and Susanna.

During our ambassador school training at the State Department, Secretary Powell met with our class and said something quite important. "If you spend all of your time with the well-connected," he told us, "you will not be representing well either me or the president." I agreed, believing it was important for the United States mission in Canada to be involved in the communities where we had a presence.

So in August 2002 we had the first US Embassy golf tournament at the Emerald Links Golf Course as a way to expand our involvement in the Ottawa community. Most importantly, we established a close relationship with Habitat for Humanity, to which the proceeds of this tournament went. Jan and I were longtime supporters of Habitat for Humanity in Massachusetts. It is well known for its work building affordable homes throughout the world for low income, hard working families. Habitat for Humanity doesn't just raise money. Habitat homes are built by the labor of the community volunteers who donate their time and bring their tools to the building sites, erecting the homes that deserving families will live in. All of the proceeds from that first US Embassy golf tournament, as well as from the 2003 and 2004 tournaments—about $16,000 in total—went to the Habitat for Humanity National Capital Region affiliate.

Our involvement with Habitat, in Ottawa and across the country, was extensive. We hosted a reception at the Residence in recognition of the volunteer staff and benefactors of Habitat's National Capital Region chapter. I was the keynote speaker at their 2003 annual gala in Ottawa, and Jan and I toured the Winnipeg facility, the first Habitat for Humanity affiliate established in Canada. Jan also did Habitat events in Vancouver, Calgary and Toronto. This was the sort of community involvement that Secretary Powell had told us was an important part of our mission. It was also something that Jan and I believed in strongly and that we had been doing for years in public life before moving to Canada.

One of the other community organizations that we supported was the Salvation Army. The embassy was active in raising money for the Ottawa chapter and Jan and I both went out on the road helping to promote the good work that the Salvation Army does. I gave a keynote speech at a fundraising event in Moncton, in support of the Atlantic region of the Salvation Army. It was the largest fundraising event ever for the Atlantic region. Jan visited their Vancouver and Calgary facilities to show our strong support for the staff and volunteers whose work is so important for Canada's neediest citizens.

As soon as I arrived in Ottawa I met Tom Higgins, an embassy employee who took me under his wing. He brought me to my first Ottawa Lynx baseball game and became my main golfing partner that first summer in Canada. More importantly, Tom was a tremendous help to me at the embassy, particularly with our law enforcement agencies and their Canadian counterparts. Our "home course" that first season was the Chateau Cartier, across the Ottawa River in Gatineau. I played many of the courses in the Ottawa area, as well as a great number of courses across Canada during my four years as ambassador. My favorites are the courses in the Canadian

Rockies—Silvertip, Banff Springs and Stewart Creek where I played a couple of rounds with Alberta Premier Ralph Klein. But the Ottawa region has some notable courses too, including Royal Ottawa, Hunt Club, Rivermead, Camelot and, of course, le Dome, now called Hautes Plaines.

I know that golf is a game. But when you play with someone, you get to know that person and bond with them in ways that help when you need to deal with them professionally. I enjoyed playing with RCMP Commissioner Giuliano Zaccardelli, Assistant Commissioner Dawson Hovey, CSIS Director Ward Elcock, Chief of the Defence Staff Ray Henault, Deputy Prime Minister John Manley, as well as many other Canadian officials with whom I developed good working relationships. I even played once with Prime Minister Chrétien. One bit of advice, though: When playing with John Manley at Camelot, and he says, "I'm walking, but you can take the cart," take the cart. The back nine is extremely hilly and Manley, a marathon runner, maneuvers across the course like a mountain goat.

After Tom Higgins left to return to his beloved New York in the summer of 2002, Richard Primeau became my main golfing partner. Richard is a successful Ottawa entrepreneur. We would often play nine holes at le Dome, teeing off at 6:00 p.m. I have to confess that he beat me every time. Pat McMurray, the embassy's secret service attaché also became a regular partner. Like Tom, he helped me enormously at work. Pat is a special person to be with on and off the golf course.

When people ask Jan and me about the highlight of our time in Ottawa, we naturally place our daughter Anne's wedding at the top of the list. She married Calgarian Craig Adams on July 26, 2003, at

Ottawa's Notre Dame Cathedral. For me, there is no more meaningful symbol of the close and permanent nature of the ties between Canada and the United States than our daughter's marriage to a Canadian. The fact that she married a hockey player was an added bonus.

Anne and Craig met when they were both students at Harvard, where Craig captained the hockey team in his senior year. They often went to a favorite Boston restaurant of mine, Filippo's, where there is a mural upstairs that features me along with the likes of Bill Clinton, Julia Child and Larry Bird. Filippo Fratarolli and his son Philip always make us feel special when we visit their restaurant.

Craig was already firmly in the picture by the time I received my posting to Canada. I remember Jan's excitement when we called him with the news. She took great pleasure in giving Craig a tour of his own capital city when he and Anne visited together for the first time. I've always been a hockey fan, and Boston is a great hockey town, so the fact that Anne was dating a hockey player gave me a welcome reason to attend some of Harvard's games. Things became complicated, though, when Craig was playing against my alma mater, Boston College. At the annual Bean Pot tournament that brings together Boston College, Boston University, Harvard and Northeastern, Anne wouldn't let me cheer for my Boston College Eagles when they were playing Harvard. This turned out to be good training for me in the divided loyalties that I would have to live with during my Ottawa years. I was a lifelong Bruins fan, but I felt I also had to support the hometown Senators.

Anne and Craig took the first major step toward their marriage when they announced their engagement at the Residence Fourth of July party in 2002. Craig had asked Anne to marry him on a beautiful June evening a few weeks earlier, proposing on the roof deck of the official residence, looking out upon the sweep of the front lawn and toward

the Ottawa River and the Gatineau Hills in the distance. I was traveling from Calgary to Toronto after seeing the president off at the end of
the G–8 summit in Kanasakis. My plan was to stay overnight at the
hotel airport in Toronto, going to Niagara Falls the next day for a Smart
Border meeting between Secretary Ridge and Minister Manley. When
I arrived in Toronto, I turned on my cell phone and found several
voicemail messages waiting for me. Then the phone rang. It was Jan
telling me to call Anne immediately. There was important news that I
needed to hear. I celebrated that evening with a drink at the Sheraton
lounge with our Toronto consul-general, Toni Marwitz. The day had
started with a farewell to the president after what we judged a successful summit and ended with wonderful family news.

Jan and I deepened our friendship with the Archbishop of the
Diocese of Ottawa, Marcel Gervais, after the terrible events of
September 11. He had provided us with comfort during those stressful days and weeks. And the Archbishop's homilies are always very
relevant to the world that we live in. His remarks at the mass on the
Sunday after the terrorist attacks were quite moving. We were
delighted when he agreed to officiate at Anne and Craig's wedding
mass in Notre Dame Cathedral on Sussex Drive, steps from the
embassy. Notre Dame Rector, Reverend Jacques Kabangu organized
and assisted in officiating on this special day at one of Canada's most
beautiful churches. Jan and I had been members of the parish from
our arrival in Ottawa, so we knew Notre Dame Cathedral well. It is
the oldest surviving church in Ottawa, built between 1841 and 1885.
The basilica's elegant twin spires are well known to all Ottawans.

I thought the time from Anne and Craig's engagement to their
wedding in the summer of 2003 flew by. Everything seemed to be
going smoothly. So smoothly that a week before their wedding day I
said to Jan and Anne, "Can I do anything to help?" They found that

enormously funny. Apparently they had made a thousand and one decisions over the previous year, getting everything ready for the big day. I felt a bit like Steve Martin in *Father of the Bride*.

But I hadn't been totally out of the loop. Anne and Jan took care of most of the planning, but I certainly paid attention to some of the details, including the guest list. Anne and Craig had expressed their desire that the wedding be a very personal affair and not a blockbuster social event. Jan and Lori Duval had created 325 handmade invitations. By Italian wedding standards this is not huge. But it still became talked about as the "social event of the season."

With guests like Prime Minister Chrétien, Andy Card, Bill Graham, John Manley, Bill Weld, and US Olympic gold skating medalist Kristi Yamaguchi as well as several NHL hockey players, it was inevitable that Anne and Craig's wedding would attract a lot of attention. I suppose the attention was also from the symbolism of the marriage of a Canadian hockey player to the daughter of the United States ambassador, bringing together two countries that were friends and neighbors, and particularly at a time when there was a lot of talk about stress in the Canada–US relationship. Everyone agreed that Anne and Craig made a striking couple.

Jan and I were especially pleased that the Chrétiens had accepted our invitation to the wedding. We had invited them as friends, people we had come to know and respect, and not out of any sense of official obligation. I know that they accepted in the same spirit and were genuinely touched to share with us this important family day.

Most Canadians and Americans have heard the voice of Canadian John McDermott. John is a great friend of ours and we were honored when he accepted our invitation to sing at the wedding. Canadians truly have a national treasure in John. He has performed before audiences around the world. In 2001, John was awarded the US Congressional Medal of Honor Society's "Bob Hope Award," one of my country's highest accolades, for his work on behalf of veterans' causes. At Anne and Craig's wedding, he sang "Panis Angelicus" and "Ave Maria" more beautifully than I've ever heard them sung.

The wedding had a strong made-in-Canada feel, from Anne's wedding gown, made by Ottawa designer Justina McCaffrey, to the Alberta beef that was served with dinner and the music of the Tragically Hip and Shania Twain that was played by an Ottawa DJ that evening. Being able to hold the reception at the Residence was a unique opportunity. We had an enormous white tent staked on the lawn for the dinner. The embassy maintenance staff rose to the occasion, as they always did, and the grounds were as beautiful as we had ever seen them.

Our Ottawa guests included Sarah Jennings and her husband Ian Johns. Many family and friends were delighted to meet the sister of one of America's most famous Canadians.

We invited many of our Massachusetts friends, along with family from Italy, England and Wales. Many of the people that I had worked with over my 30 years in Massachusetts politics were there to share this special day with us, including my former boss, Governor Bill Weld; my former legal counsel Len Lewin and his wife, Ellen; my former chief of staff Virginia Buckingham and her husband, Judge David Lowy; my former campaign manager and current media advisor Rob Gray and his wife, Karyn; Steve O'Neill, who had started with me as my campaign advance person and rose to become my chief of staff when I was governor, and his wife, Kelly O'Neill, who had been my longtime personal assistant. Mary Lee and Richard King, my high school classmate, were also there. Mary Lee had assisted on all my state election campaigns from the very first one in 1976. Jim and Paula Connolly also made the trip to Ottawa. Jim had led the fundraising effort for my successful 1998 run for the governorship, and Paula is one of Jan's closest friends. Robert Platt, who had helped Jim raise campaign money for me in Massachusetts, and his wife, Shelly, were there to share the special day with us. Our friends Peter and Gail Lewenberg, and Ralph and Deb Sbrogna also joined us. Our daughter Anne was so very happy that my State Police detail from Massachusetts came to her wedding. Jim Hanifin, Anthony Dichio, Steve Howard, John McGuire and John Cahill had come to be like members of our family when I was governor. Being able to share this special day with people that I had known and worked with for so long was a blessing. After dinner, Andy Card, Andrew Natsios, Leon Lombardi, and I—George H. W. Bush's "four horsemen" from the 1980 campaign—along with our "rider" Ron Kaufman, had a celebratory cigar together. It was a day that I could have only imagined 30 years earlier, when I started out as a local politician in Hudson.

The only note of sadness in what otherwise was a perfect day was the fact that Anne's maternal grandfather and Craig's maternal grandfather were not able to be there. Their medical conditions made it impossible for either of them to travel so far. It gave a bittersweet note to the day, not having two of the grandparents there to share such a joyous occasion, when these two young people were starting their life together.

———————————

Fourth of July parties are a great tradition at the ambassador's official residence. We enjoyed every one of the four parties that we were privileged to host. Each was different and each was memorable in its own way. There were always described by local media scribes as the "hottest ticket in town."

Jan and I wanted to honor veterans at the 2003 Independence Day celebrations. Our country was at war and it was only fitting that the sacrifices that the men and women of the military have made, and continue to make, in defense of freedom be recognized on a day that commemorates our forefathers' fight for freedom. We had over 2,500 guests at the Residence for the 2003 Independence Day party, on a typical hot, humid Ottawa summer day. The honored veterans arrived first. Jan and I greeted every one of them personally. Jan got a lot of endearing smiles and warm expressions of appreciation that day, as well as a few hugs and kisses, a new book on Canadian military history, three phone numbers, an offer of a dinner date, and two pinches. I got lots of smiles and expressions of appreciation, but no pinches. There were over 100 veterans from World War II, the Korean War and the Vietnam War. Our special guest of honor was Ottawa resident Paul Métivier, who was Canada's oldest living World War I veteran. "I'm overcome," he said, dressed in his blue blazer decorated with service medals and a banded straw hat. "I enlisted at 16 years of age and I outlived all my family, and here I am almost 103 and look at all the fuss that is going on." Mr. Métivier turned 103 two days later.

In my remarks that day, which I kept brief in deference to the sweltering weather, I praised Canada's military contributions over the years. "One of the great symbols of the enduring friendship between Canada and the United States," I said, "is our veterans, because they have fought together on the beaches of Normandy, in the hills of Korea, in the hills of Italy, in the mountains of Afghanistan, on the waves of the Persian Gulf, and, today, they are together in the command center at NORAD."

Tenor John McDermott is well known for his work on behalf of veterans. We were grateful to have him with us that day to serenade the honored soldiers with musical tributes to their valor and bravery. John sang the World War I ballad "Willy McBride," "Shenandoah" and an emotional rendition of "America the Beautiful." He and the veterans chatted well into the evening and he signed hundreds of autographs.

After the last guests departed, Jan and I hosted a reception in the Residence for the hot and exhausted members of the various security agencies that had worked throughout the long day to ensure the safety of our guests and our large staff. It was fascinating to hear them talk about the innovative crowd-control tactics that they had used to handle the protestors who had appeared outside the gates of the Residence. When Jan heard about how profusely the officers sweated from wearing their bulletproof vest in the steamy heat, she said that perhaps we all should have worn them. Then we could have grazed all afternoon at the buffet table, nibbling the magnificent creations and not gained an ounce!

A presidential visit is always special. The embassy personnel and residence staff, models of professionalism at all times, seem to find an extra gear when the president is in town.

Jan and I had been looking forward to hosting President Bush and the First Lady since our arrival in Ottawa. The president had visited Canada on two occasions, in Quebec at a meeting of the Summit of the Americas in 2001, and at Kananaskis for the G–8 meeting in June of 2002. And he had planned to come to Ottawa in May 2003, but postponed that visit when the timing turned out not to be right. Both the president and Prime Minister Martin were keen to organize a formal state visit to Canada. Once President Bush won re-election on November 2, 2004, this visit became a priority for both governments.

When Prime Minister Martin telephoned President Bush to congratulate him on his election victory, he also invited him to Ottawa. Then the behind-the-scenes work of organizing everything from security to a gala state dinner for 700 people at the Museum of Civilization began.

When Air Force One touched down in Ottawa on November 30, Jan and I were there to welcome President and Mrs. Bush to Canada. Winter already had Ottawa in its grip. The temperature hovered around 0° Celsius and several inches of snow would fall that night. Jan and I were well acclimatized to the Ottawa weather and so we thought nothing of running up the stairs into Air Force One coatless. President Bush noticed my new Canali suit and said, "Celooch, you've gone European on us!" "It's an Italian suit, Mr. President, and I'm an Italian." Once again, the president showed his eye for detail.

The president and his entourage had seen the temperature reading and were unconvinced by our bravado in going without coats and hats. They bundled up before deplaning, then off we went by motorcade to Parliament Hill.

As we made our way into the city, the president asked me question after question on issues from the cattle embargo to missile defense. I couldn't help but recall our official visit to Israel, where Governor Bush had shown a keen interest and a sharp appreciation of the political issues explained to us by our Israeli hosts. As long as I have known him, the president has been interested in foreign affairs. I could tell that he had been well briefed and that he had a solid grasp of the issues that his Canadian hosts would want to talk about.

Ottawans are a hardy lot, and there were thousands of them along the route leading to Parliament. Most of them were well-wishers, waving as the presidential motorcade passed by. There were, of course, some protestors, as there are whenever and wherever an

American president travels. One group of particularly vitriolic demonstrators seemed quite perplexed when the president smiled broadly and waved to them. But, as the president said afterward when thanking Canadians for their warm hospitality on that cold day, most of those waving used all five fingers.

When the president's Ottawa itinerary was being planned, Jan had pushed hard for a visit to the National Library and the Archives Preservation Centre in Gatineau, just across the Ottawa River in Quebec. In fact, we could see the Preservation Centre from the north-facing side of the Residence. I confess that I had my doubts. But in the end Jan prevailed and on the afternoon of their visit we accompanied the president and first lady on a library and archive tour. On the way into the archive building I couldn't resist saying to President Bush, "This was Jan's idea." As it turns out, I should have taken some credit for the visit. The president loved it. He was fascinated by an old French map, dating from 1698, that showed California as an island! On the drive back to Ottawa, he talked enthusiastically about the building's structure and layout and said that it had furthered his thinking about his eventual presidential library.

Before going to the state dinner that evening we relaxed for an hour at the Residence. The president and I went directly to the library where we talked about family, and sports. I think he may have spotted my copy of the *Boston Globe*'s commemorative book on the Red Sox 2004 World Series–winning season. I left it prominently displayed on an end table so that everyone could be reminded of my team's magical season.

I was very pleased that our daughter Anne and our cousin from Italy, Susanna Cellucci, came to stay with us during the president's visit. President and Mrs. Bush have a strong sense of family and I know they welcomed the warmth and exuberance that the presence of younger Celluccis brought to our home. When it was time to drive from the Residence to the Museum of Civilization for dinner, the president invited them to ride in his limousine. They looked as though they had just arrived from Milan, the fashion capital of the world, which was in fact where they had arrived from. In elegant dresses and high heels, Anne balanced on the limousine's console between the president and Mrs. Bush while Susanna was perched precariously between Jan and me. We made it to the dinner without either the president or me stepping on their dresses.

Laura Bush had to return to Washington after the state dinner, but the president, Condi Rice and Andy Card stayed the night at our place. With a small army of security and support staff inside and outside the house, we all slept soundly through the wintry night. It snowed overnight and when the president came down for breakfast on the terrace the next morning I said to him, "Isn't this a beautiful winter wonderland?" In true Texan fashion he replied, "It is, if you like snow." But I'm sure President Bush was impressed by the beauty of Ottawa covered in a blanket of white. Jan and I felt a strong pride in being able to show off this city that we had come to think of as home.

Postscript:

During the presidential visit to Ottawa, President Bush's personal aide, Blake Gottesman, had remarked to Jan that he knew how overwhelming such a visit to an official residence can be. "Blake," Jan replied, "this still doesn't rise to the level of the Cellucci family arriving for Christmas."

CHAPTER TEN

From Coast to Coast to Coast

During my years as ambassador, one of the great joys was to visit every part of Canada, to see its beauty and meet its people. That was the other side of public diplomacy. Not only did I choose to speak out, explaining my government's view of the world and of Canada, but I chose to visit communities all across the country. So public diplomacy was a happy marriage of business and pleasure. There was hardly a week when we were not traveling outside of Ottawa, often to several communities in a single week. Our travels took us from Alert, Nunavut in the North to Pelee Island, Ontario, in the South, from Beaver Creek, Yukon in the West to St. John's, Newfoundland in the East.

John Kenneth Galbraith had urged me to see the country and the people beyond the capital, and that's what I did. We were lucky in that we got to see much more of the country than most Canadians get to see, traveling to every corner and meeting people from all walks of life. And we came to appreciate Pierre Trudeau's reflection on the importance of land to the Canadian identity:

I know a man who never learned patriotism in school, but who acquired that virtue when he felt in his bones the vastness of his land and the greatness of its founders.

Jan chronicled our travels and activities in the column she wrote for the *Maple Leaf*, the newspaper for the embassy community. The column made its way to the US consulates across Canada as well as to the Canada desk at the State Department and Canada's Department of Foreign Affairs. It was a great success because it let everyone know what we had been up to, where, and how we felt about it, all through the lens of Jan's irreverent perspective on the world and her husband. Reading through the hundreds of pages Jan wrote I am once more surprised by how much we did, by all the places we saw, and by all the people we met. I'd like to share some of them.

Canadians have a great sense of humor, and Atlantic Canadians are second to none in their love of a good laugh. I discovered just how funny they can be on one of my trips to Halifax, not long after I took up the post. I was in town to give a speech to the Metropolitan Halifax Chamber of Commerce. Jan says that my notes for this talk seemed to have been scribbled with a crayon and that my messy scrawl was visible through the Plexiglas lectern. But I guess people were so spellbound by my speech that she was the only one to notice this.

Later that evening I was ambushed. I had been told what was coming, but nothing fully prepares you for a face-to-face encounter with Mary Walsh of *This Hour Has 22 Minutes*. She was doing her Connie Bloor persona—the full Mary Walsh performance. I figured that I was in for it, and I was right.

Ambassador Paul Cellucci during break at Global Business Forum in Banff, Alberta, September 26, 2002.(*CP PHOTO/ADRIAN WYLD*)

Security Trumps Trade. Ambassador Paul Cellucci speaks at Economic Club of Toronto, March 25, 2003, just after the Canadian government decides not to support US in Iraq. (*CP PHOTO/FRANK GUNN*)

Ambassador Paul Cellucci and Governor Jeb Bush of Florida launch the American Chamber of Commerce in Canada, in Toronto, Ontario, July 8, 2003. (*CP PHOTO/ KEVIN FRAYER*)

Ambassador Paul Cellucci throws out the first pitch prior to the Texas Rangers vs. Toronto Blue Jays game in Toronto, Ontario, April 29, 2003. Sending message that Toronto is safe despite SARS. (© *PHOTO BY SYSTEM 4 PRODUCTIONS INC.*)

Discussion on US–Canada relations. Ambassador Paul Cellucci and Canadian Consul General to New York Pamela Wallin at Radio–Television News Directors Association convention in Halifax, Nova Scotia, June 20, 2003. (*CP PHOTO/ANDREW VAUGHN*)

Anne Cellucci with her maid of honor, Kate Cellucci, prior to the ceremony. (*ANTHONY CAVA, PHOTUX STUDIO, OTTAWA, ON*)

Anne and Craig with Prime Minister Jean Chrétien and Aline Chrétien. (*ANTHONY CAVA, PHOTUX STUDIO, OTTAWA, ON*)

The Cellucci family. (*ANTHONY CAVA, PHOTUX STUDIO, OTTAWA, ON*)

Ambassador Paul Cellucci escorts daughter Anne into Notre Dame Cathedral. (*CP PHOTO/CHRIS WATTIE*)

Mr. and Mrs. Craig Adams, the newly-weds. (*ANTHONY CAVA, PHOTUX STUDIO, OTTAWA, ON*)

Ambassador Paul Cellucci presents Marley Leger with a Bronze Star posthumously for her husband Sgt. Leger during a ceremony in Edmonton, Alberta, December 8, 2003. (*CP PHOTO/ADRIAN WYLD*)

Craig Adams after scoring his first NHL goal. Raleigh, North Carolina, November 10, 2002. (© *CAROLINA HURRICANES*)

Ambassador Paul Cellucci and Prime Minister Paul Martin chat while they attend the 400th anniversary of the French on L'Ille-Sainte-Croix, in Bayside, New Brunswick, June 26, 2004. (*CP PHOTO/TOM HANSON*)

Irish tenor John McDermott, Ambassador Paul Cellucci, Italian Ambassador Marco Colombo, Mexican Ambassador to Canada Maria-Theresa de Madero, and British High Commissioner David Redeway at Ottawa Senators hockey game.

Ginny Devine, Premier Gary Doer, Ambassador Paul Cellucci, and Jan Cellucci touring Churchill, Manitoba, October 22, 2004. (© *MIKE MACRI, MACRI PHOTO AND DESIGN*)

Jan and Paul Cellucci fly fishing in the Restigouche River, New Brunswick, August 12, 2004. (*PHOTO BY YVAN LONG*)

"Tex" Cellucci, Calgary Stampede Parade, July 9, 2004. (*PHOTO BY BETTY RICE*)

Red Sox finally win the World Series and Tom Higgins, die-hard New York Yankees' fan, pays in New York City, November 2004. (*PHOTO BY FIONA HIGGINS*)

Canada's new ambassador to the United States Frank McKenna, and Deputy US Ambassador to Canada Paul Cellucci at new conference on counter terrorism in Ottawa, March 17, 2005. (*CP PHOTO/TOM HANSON*)

If that isn't Paul Cellucci, the United States Ambassador to Canada! And run me back and forth buck naked across the longest undefended border in the world, and make me sing "Fifty four-Forty or Fight" until I fall down in a patriotic fervor, eh? How about that harmonization, eh? Where the Canadian mouse and the Manifest Destiny elephant are to be one in the biblical sense. Oh say, that's really gonna hurt the mouse, eh? We'll have to wrap the whole country in duct tape.

Mr. Ambassador?

"Yes?"

Connie Bloor, sir. [snort, snort] I gotta admit, first when I heard about Fortress North America, erasing the borders and joining our two countries together, I gotta admit I was a bit frightened, eh? But then I adjusted my medication and now I'm good with it and I think that if that's what it takes to be secure then, well . . .

"But maybe the US will become the 11th Canadian province."

Okay, you can be the 11th province, sir. Well, you're a bit big to be a province, but maybe a territory, okay? And, well, I'm here tonight as a sort of federal welcome wagon and I just brought you this [reaches into coat pocket and pulls out a red toque shaped like a maple leaf]. *It's a toque. Go ahead, put it on. Once you become the 11th province it's kind of do reeger (de riguer).*

[Connie starts to sing] *Oh Canada, our home's on native land!*

I actually liked the toque and I still have it. But I didn't put it on when we were on camera, despite Connie's urging. It was not that I thought it would diminish the dignity of my role as ambassador, although that certainly would have been the result. It was just that I got a frightening vision of the picture on the front page of the next day's papers—Connie Bloor in her lumberjack shirt and toque, looking like one of the Mackenzie brothers, and me in a bright red toque shaped like a pointy leaf. I though I might have a hard time maintaining the respect of my staff after that.

———————————

Our consuls-general dutifully learned to consult the NHL schedule as soon as it was released each summer. Visiting the consulates, from Vancouver to Halifax, was an important part of my job. So why not time my trips to coincide with my son-in-law's hockey games in Canada? By the time I left my post, I had seen Craig play in every Canadian NHL rink except in his hometown of Calgary. Our consul-genreal in Montreal, Bernadette Allen, saw us frequently as that great city is only two hours by car from Ottawa.

On one occasion my cousin Ornella Palieri, her husband Pietro, and daughter Ilaria, were visiting us in Ottawa. We wanted to take them to their first hockey game, to get a full introduction to Canada. As luck had it, we were invited to a playoff game in Montreal against Craig's Carolina Hurricanes, as guests of the Canadiens' owner, George Gillette. He is from Colorado and is as intense a hockey fan as you'll find. With his team up 3 to 0 halfway through the third period, Mr. Gillette was obviously feeling confident about the game. The Hurricanes had their chances but just couldn't put the puck in the net. Then the drama began. Montreal was penalized with about 10 minutes to go. The Canadiens' coach, Michel Therrien, protested a little too much for the referee's liking and received a bench penalty. With a five on three advantage, the Hurricanes quickly scored. They added two more goals before the end of the period, sending it into overtime. You could feel the momentum shift to the visiting team. The Hurricanes went on to win in overtime and would eventually go on to play the Detroit Red Wings in that season's Stanley Cup final. Even as the game slipped away from the Canadiens, Mr. Gillette remained a gentleman and a gracious host—and for Ornella, Pietro and Ilaria, their introduction to hockey was an extraordinary game.

———————

When someone in Massachusetts says that they're going north for the weekend people assume that they mean to the seaside in Maine or maybe skiing in New Hampshire. A trip as far as Quebec City would be considered seriously north. But I quickly discovered that the North means something very different in Canada. Beyond the tree line and long past where the road ends, that's really up north.

Some of my fondest memories of Canada are of my trips above the Arctic Circle. You don't get farther north than Alert in Nunavut, the northernmost inhabited settlement in the world. Jan and I started our odyssey at Trenton Air Base on a C-130 Hercules to Thule Air Base in Greenland. There, about 800 military personnel from Canada, the United States and Denmark operate a highly sophisticated missile warning, space surveillance, and satellite tracking and control center on the roof of the world. The C-130 Hercules is a transport workhorse. Forget about business class. We were strapped in amidst all sorts of cargo and given earplugs for the eight hour flight to Thule, with a refueling stop in Iqaluit.

Traveling with us was Vermont's governor, Howard Dean, who at the time was considering a run for the presidency. We had been New England governors together, and we got on quite well despite our party differences. In 1997 the Massachusetts state senate was considering a bill that would have taken the state out of the New England Dairy Compact, a move that would have caused serious damage to the region's dairy industry, particularly in Vermont. Governor Dean called looking for help. "Don't worry," I told him, "I'm going to step outside my office after I get off the phone and let the Senate know that I'll veto any attempt to take Massachusetts out of the Dairy Compact." I had enough votes in the Senate to sustain a veto, so the legislation died. Governor Dean was very grateful. Although he was the member of the Democratic National Governors Association charged with helping to elect new Democratic governors across the country, I noticed that he didn't come to Massachusetts during the 1998 gubernatorial campaign.

We stayed overnight at Thule, then flew to Alert, situated on the northeastern tip of Ellesmere Island, about 500 miles from the geographic North Pole and more than 1,800 miles north of the closest inhabited settlement. It was early August and the weather was glorious—some of the time. One day it was 50° Fahrenheit, about 10° Celsius, under the brilliant sun of an Arctic summer. We saw huge Arctic hares and, crazily perhaps, walked barefoot in the Arctic Ocean. The next day we hiked through a blowing snowstorm. It is a part of the country that I wish every Canadian could see. We trekked across a tundra riverbed to an ice cave, dug for crystals on a frigid, barren mountaintop, and saw icebergs of spectacular beauty and variety. We ate our meals in The Igloo Gardens, the most northerly dining room in the world.

And we became "blue noses." It is a navy tradition that anyone crossing the Arctic Circle for the first time has his nose daubed blue. The blue is, of course, a symbol of the cold. So Jan and I, and one of the men who wanted to challenge my boss for the presidency of the United States in the 2004 election, happily submitted to this initiation into the circle of those who have been privileged to visit the high Arctic.

The next evening, at a dinner in our honor, the Canadian Forces served Chateaubriand from Alberta and lobster tails from Cuba. Fine dining in the far north. I said a few words thanking the Canadian government and forces for maintaining this important facility. Alert is a listening post equipped like a small city that supports the seven engineers who operate the signal system. The local airport is Alert's lifeline to the world, the only way in and out because it is thousands of miles from the nearest road and shifting icepacks make the sea impossible to navigate. There is a power plant, a water treatment facility, a medical clinic, an impressive recreational center and, of course, The Igloo Gardens restaurant. It is extraordinarily expensive to maintain this facility at such a remote location.

As I concluded my remarks, I mentioned that Governor Dean was thinking of running for president against my boss. "We have the photos from the blue nose ceremony," I warned him, "and we won't hesitate to use them if your candidacy takes off. We'll say, 'This guy might be fun to have at a party, but do you really want him to be president of the United States?'"

When it was time to leave, we boarded another C-130 Hercules and strapped ourselves in lengthwise along benches of orange nylon webbing, facing ominously labeled Arctic Survival kits mounted on the wall. But at Thule they told us that another C-130, scheduled to fly us the last leg of the trip back to Trenton, had a broken propeller. So we had to settle for a Canadian Forces Airbus, with leather seats, paneled walls, a shower, a full-course meal, and no earplugs. We finally arrived back at the Residence late that evening, having slept the previous night in a dorm bed thousands of miles away. We fell asleep with a memory that we will always cherish, of a part of Canada whose pristine beauty is beyond compare.

For spectacular, timeless beauty, there is nothing like the temperate rain forests of the British Columbia coast. Jan and I traveled to Canada's Pacific coast often, but one of our most memorable trips was to the Queen Charlotte Islands (Haida Gwaii), off the northern coast of British Columbia, just south of the Alaska panhandle. The archipelago of 138 islands is the ancestral home of the Haida people, a breathtaking meeting of land and sea, abundant wildlife, and a resurgent Haida culture. Much of the islands' beauty comes from the stark contrasts—wild, open seas and calm, secluded bays, towering forests on the mountainsides, thundering surf coming in from the oceans, heavy skies dropping cold rain, then the sun transforming the colors of forest and sea. It is truly one of the jewels of Canada's natural heritage.

Jan and I and our consul-general in Vancouver, Luis Arreaga, and his wife, Mary, had been invited as guests of the Skidegate Band Council, the largest Haida community in Haida Gwaii. Our guide was Guujaw, president of the Council of Haida Nations. He has a straight-spoken manner and I liked him immediately. Guujaw said the Haida had thrived on the islands for more than 10,000 years before their numbers were decimated by epidemics brought by Europeans. We traveled with Guujaw by floatplane to SGang Gwaay, the furthest tip of the islands and the place most sacred to the Haida. He guided us along the trails through the forests to the Haida totem poles, explaining the natural habitat and recounting the legends of his people.

Miles Richardson graciously offered his mother's home for our accommodations and one evening Jan and I were the guests of the

Skidegate Band at an island camp, with crashing seas around us and bald eagles soaring overhead where we soaked luxuriously in the Hot Springs. I went long-line fishing with Haida Chief Willard Wilson. We caught halibut and red snapper that day, and cooked them over the fire that evening. The weather was beautiful, getting into the 80s and sunny—a lucky break for a place that gets more rain than any part of Canada.

We ate delicious meals, including the fish we had caught that day, and the only thing missing was dessert. As it happened, a Canadian Coast Guard vessel was anchored nearby, just off Hot Springs Island. Some of the Haida went out to the vessel and bartered a halibut for freshly cooked brownies. They were delicious.

Calgary is a vibrant city that I came to love during my years in Canada. Among the people that I got to know well was the mayor, David Bronconnier, who became my golfing partner whenever the weather cooperated. So I was pleased when I got a call from him in April 2004. My thought was that we might be able to get together for another round of golf before I left my post, but David had something else in mind.

He invited me to ride in the Calgary Stampede. The complication was that I needed to ride a horse, something I'd never done in my life. But this sounded like too much fun to pass up, so I called another golfing partner, Zack, RCMP Commissioner Giuliano Zaccardelli, and he arranged to have me take riding lessons at the RCMP stables, about a mile from my residence. So once a week, for eight weeks, at 6:30 in the morning, Bill Stewart, the ride master, gave me riding lessons. We started inside and then, as the weather warmed and I grew more confident in the saddle, the lessons moved outdoors. I even rode with

Zack, who is an accomplished horseman. Those who have seen the RCMP horses in Ottawa will know that they are big, very big. I trained on Dawn and Vito, two good-tempered and beautiful animals that made me feel like I was born for the saddle.

Jan was skeptical about my horsemanship, despite the stories of progress that I would bring home. I could have asked her to come along at 6:30 in the morning to watch as I rode around the stable grounds, but then I came up with another idea. One Saturday morning I left the residence on my way to the stables, telling the guard at the gate that I'd be back in an hour. We had house guests that weekend, Jan's cousin Tom Kline and his wife, Beth Kline, and their daughter Kirsten, and Jan's friend Donna Ferullo, so I knew that I'd have several witnesses to what I had in mind. Bill Stewart and I got our horses ready, then headed through the streets of Rockcliffe toward the residence. Once there, the driveway to the house rises and curves on a hill. I asked the guard to call Jan to tell her that a "special delegation from the RCMP" was arriving. Just as we reached the crest of the hill, in view of the residence, Jan saw me on horseback. She is seldom speechless, but for a brief instant that day words failed her.

When we got to Calgary the day before the Stampede parade, I was given a smaller horse than I had trained on. His name was Danny. My schedule allowed a day for me to get used to him, and him to me, before I had to ride in front of thousands of people along the parade route. Danny and the other Stampede horses are often used in movies, so he was quite ready for the parade. I was a bit more nervous, knowing that I would be before my son-in-law's home town, with his family in the stands, as well as Jan, Kate and Anne. Our consul-general Naim Ahmed, his wife Linda and the Calgary consulate staff would also be watching.

Danny took the bit in his mouth and I strapped on my Calgary police services belt buckle, white Stetson and cowboy shirt, and we did just fine. In other words, I managed the two-and-a-half-hour parade route without falling off, which I count as a success. I was sore at the end of it, but I think I served my country well. To make the experience complete, Craig took us to the notorious Cowboys bar were we celebrated in high style. Jan claims that she had to drag Tex Cellucci out of the place, but how often do you get to ride in the Calgary Stampede?

Toronto was a frequent destination during my four years in Canada. I visited the city over 40 times and came to know it very well. I know that Torontonians are very proud of their city and think of it as world class. They are right. It is dynamic and at the same time livable, economically vibrant and culturally diverse. It is a city with something for everyone and it is a favorite destination for American tourists. When the SARS crisis hit in 2003 and the tourists stopped coming for fear of catching the virus, the city had to re-establish public confidence in Toronto as a safe place to visit. Paul Godfrey, president and CEO of the Blue Jays baseball team, called and asked me to throw out the first pitch at a game against the Texas Rangers. He was hoping that my willingness to be there would further reassure fans watching the game on television in Canada and the United States that Toronto was a safe city. Jan found this very funny, the idea that my presence would reassure anyone that a place was safe. But it was one piece in the bigger public relations campaign that the city undertook to dispel the cloud of fear that hung over Toronto during those months. I threw a nice strike right down the heart of the plate.

I came back to Toronto two months later with Florida Governor Jeb Bush to deliver the same message of reassurance. Governor Bush was very aware of the importance of the Canadian "snowbirds" to his state's economy and wanted to show solidarity with Torontonians during their difficult time. We also kicked off the opening of the American Chamber of Commerce in Canada while he was in town, yet another sign of the close economic ties between the world's greatest trading partners.

I was in Toronto quite a lot during the months of the SARS crisis. A week after Anne and Craig's wedding there was a SARS benefit concert in Toronto, with the Rolling Stones as the headliners. Kate and her friend Shaun Donovan wanted to go, so we arranged to stay with our consul-general, Toni Marwitz, and go to the concert the next day. It was a remarkable event. Half a million people from all over Canada and the United States, spread over a huge field in Downsview, were dramatic evidence Toronto was safe for visitors. Once again Senator Grafstein along with member of Parliament Dennis Mills led the charge organizing this huge event. I'm not exactly a fan of the Stones' music, but I had a good time.

If not a Stones fan, I am a serious movie buff. During my years as governor of Massachusetts I would issue my "Top 10" list every year, published in the *Boston Herald*. During our years in Ottawa my list of favorites was published annually in Jan's "Maple Leaf" column. It happened that I was in Toronto on business in September 2002, when the Toronto Film Festival was taking place, so Jan and I and Anne and her friend Laura Winthrop, one of John Kerry's cousins, took the opportunity to go to the films every evening. We attended the première of Edoardo Ponti's *Between Strangers*, starring his mother, Sophia Loren, and the North American premiere of *Femme Fatale*. The leading actress in *Femme Fatale*, Rebecca Romijn-Stamos, plays a thief in Paris who double-crosses some nasty characters and has to flee the city. She returns years later as the wife of the United States ambassador to Paris and tries to keep a low profile so as not to be recognized. But when a paparazzi takes her photo, blowing her cover, she wants to leave Paris. When she disappears, the authorities think that she has been kidnapped. But she has told the paparazzi—played by Antonio Banderas—that she was leaving because her husband beats her. He tells this later to a Paris police officer questioning him about her disappearance. Then the officer says incredulously, "Do you really expect us to believe that the American ambassador beats his wife?" I burst out laughing, the only one in the theater to do so. I felt the heat of Jan's silent stare. After the screening we went to the reception and Rebecca Romijn-Stamos was there. I went up to her and said, "I'm the American ambassador." Anne stayed right next to me, making sure she didn't have her eye on another American ambassador.

North West River is near Goose Bay at the center of Labrador, at the upper end of Hamilton Inlet. Jan and I were privileged to be the guests of the Sheshatshiu Innu First Nation, who had elected its first female band chief just months before our visit. Chief Anastasia Qupee made her first public speech—ever—while we were in Goose Bay. It was direct, heartfelt and moving. I'd like to share it:

> It is an honor to welcome visitors to our homeland, and this morning I want to especially welcome Ambassador Cellucci, representing all the people of the United States of America.
>
> Until a very recent time, all my people, the Innu, were nomadic hunters who lived and traveled year round throughout this beautiful land. My parents rarely see visitors, but I

know they would show Ambassador and Mrs. Cellucci respect and kindness if they met them, sharing with them whatever food and shelter they have.

In most ways, the world we live in today is dramatically different from the world of my parents. While my parents still live their lives isolated from other cultures, it is impossible for my children growing up Innu today to remain isolated from the rest of the world.

We need to strengthen our connections with others outside our culture, outside this province, in fact outside Canada, because when it comes down to it, no matter what our culture, or what our country, I really believe we share the same basic desire and that is for their future. To make this happen we need to share knowledge, ideas and understanding across all our borders.

I am very glad you are able to come to our beautiful part of the world to learn from us and help us learn from you. I hope you will visit us again.

I have fishing stories from both coasts of Canada. Months after dropping the line in the Pacific with Chief Wilson, Jan and I were invited by New Brunswick Premier Bernard Lord and his wife, Diane, to Larry's Gulch, the province's official fishing lodge. Premier Jean Charest and his wife, Michèle Dionne, Premier Gary Doer and his wife, Ginny Devine, and Pam Wallin, Canada's consul-general in New York, were also there for a three days of fly-fishing. This was new to me. I had seen fly-fishing in movies, but I had never tried my hand at it before that trip. I thought that my hosts had an unfair advantage over me.

Whoever said that the fish are more likely to bite when it's raining hasn't been to Larry's Gulch. It rained most of the time we were there, alternating between heavy downpours and drizzle. In two days of fishing only one fish was caught. I caught it. I thought that I detected some grumpiness and mild resentment from three very competitive premiers, all of whom are respectable outdoorsmen, but who came away empty-handed while the rookie fly-fisherman from the States carried off the only trophy. We had a good time, though, the uncooperative fish and less-than-ideal weather notwithstanding.

Jan sensed that the fish weren't biting. She spent a lot of time in the rustic lodge. It is the sort of place that is an ideal escape from the fast-paced rhythm of city life. There was a lot of conversation, but apparently lots of time for reading too. The best part of our trip was the conversations at meal times. We tried to solve all of the major political issues in our two countries, and some international ones as well. Thinking back on our years in Canada, some of the best times that we had were in the company of the premiers, that fishing trip to Larry's Gulch included.

Diamond Tooth Gertie's sounds like the sort of place your mother warned you to stay away from. It is a Klondike-style saloon in Dawson City, a town of 1,800 people, in the Yukon Territory. Jan and I visited Dawson City and its landmark saloon a year after I took up my post. We were there for the Conference of the Western Premiers and Governors, which annually brings together the premiers of the four Western provinces, the leaders of the three territories, and some Western governors. Governors Tony Knowles of Alaska and Jim Geringer of Wyoming were at the Dawson City conference, as was

Michael Kergin, Canada's ambassador to Washington. Our counsel-general in Vancouver, Hugo Lorens, set this trip up.

We were there in June, when the sun still shines at midnight. That first evening, with only the clock to tell us that it was in fact approaching the end of the day, several of us went to Diamond Tooth Gertie's to experience the local culture. We weren't disappointed. The honky-tonk piano, saloon dance-hall girls and roulette table felt like something out of gold rush times. Dawson was, of course, the center of the Klondike Gold Rush over a hundred years ago, immortalized by such writers as Canada's Pierre Berton and my country's Jack London. Jan visited the Jack London cabin and museum in Dawson.

One of the traditions in Dawson City is to take a drink with a human toe in the glass. And to do it right, so that it counts, you have to let your lips touch the toe as you drink. Premiers Doer and Campbell were up to the challenge, but when it came my turn I said, "The only foot that I put in my mouth is my own!" I never did find out where the toe came from.

I love golf, but I never imagined that I would need my golf clubs on a trip north of the Arctic Circle. To my amazement, I played a round of midnight golf at the Top of the World golf course. Forget tundra and muskeg, this golf course has real grass fairways and greens. It was another truly memorable Canadian experience.

After the conference, Jan and I spent a day driving north from Dawson City to the Arctic Circle. When we finally got there, it was 72° Fahrenheit and sunny. Not the place of wind and frostbite that we had envisioned. The Yukon government provided a helicopter to take us back over the rugged terrain and desolate mountains to Dawson. We tried to imagine traveling this harsh, dramatic landscape on foot or by dogsled, as the first North-West Mounted Police had done while settling the territory. The next day, we traveled on the Top of the World Highway to the northernmost border crossing between the United States and Canada, at Poker Creek. This joint facility is shared and administered by Canadian and US immigration and customs officials. It includes housing cabins and its own power-generating facility. Then, after driving five more hours on the Alaska Highway and before re-entering Canada, we visited the Alcan border facility. On Sunday, we hiked in the glorious Kluane National Park in the Yukon and then drove to Whitehorse, meeting Yukon Premier Pat Duncan for dinner. We listened with great interest to her dreams for her territory and to her analysis of the unique challenges facing government in the Far North.

Jan and I have a special place in our hearts for Gander and the other Canadian communities that welcomed American air travelers in their hour of need. On the first anniversary of the September 11 attacks, I traveled with Prime Minister Chrétien to a commemorative ceremony at Gander International Airport, where 38 of the diverted commercial planes landed. The warm welcome the stranded passengers received in this small community of 9,600 people has since become a lasting metaphor for the role that Canada has long played in the world community. Many of those passengers returned to Gander that day to express their personal thanks to the community that received them like family.

In my speech, I tried to express the gratitude that my president and the American people felt toward the people of Gander and Canada. But I also talked about the challenge that our countries would continue to face, and how important it is that freedom-loving countries like ours face it shoulder to shoulder.

Today, we remember most of all the lives lost, and the families that were shattered. Our prayers and best wishes go out to those who continue to bear the greatest loss.

We also remember with great gratitude Canada's overwhelming help, and support to the United States in our time of need. Within minutes of the attacks the prime minister called our embassy to offer whatever was necessary. Shortly thereafter planes began to land here in Gander, and all across Canada. Here you opened your schools, your churches, your homes, and you opened your hearts. I am proud to be with the people of Gander today. This basic human kindness was seen all over Canada.

I will never forget the memorial outside of the Parliament Buildings on September 14th. We are grateful for the humanitarian assistance Canadians provided to New York City and Washington, DC. We are grateful for the extraordinary cooperation between Canadian and US intelligence and law enforcement agencies tracking down terrorists here in North America. We have built a zone of confidence in North America, and a Smart Border between the US and Canada, *une frontière ouverte au commerce mais fermée aux terroristes*. And of course, we are most grateful to the Canadian military for its outstanding efforts in fighting the war in Afghanistan. We continue to mourn the four soldiers lost in the friendly fire incident; but we honor them and their comrades for their commitment to freedom.

So I come to Gander to say: Thank you, Gander. Thank you, Canada.

But we must also remember our work is not done. Much has been accomplished during the last year in the campaign

against terrorism. This struggle will require vigilance, perseverance, and sacrifice for many years to come. Canada and
the United States must continue to work as partners, and
great friends in the days, weeks, months and years ahead to
defeat global terrorism, maintain our way of life, and build a
bright future for our children."

When you travel as much as Jan and I do, lost luggage is no surprise.
So when we flew to Iqaluit for a three-day trip with our Quebec City
consul-general, Abigail Friedman, we were not particularly surprised
when our luggage didn't arrive with us. I picked up a couple of things
at Arctic Adventures, an aptly named store, and Jan and Abby washed
their clothes in the hotel sinks.

Iqaluit is the capital of Nunavut, and has a population of 6,000.
The city is home to the Territorial Legislative Assembly, the only hospital in a territory which makes up close to one-fifth of Canada's land
mass, a college, an international airport, a museum, gravel roads,
hotels and restaurants, a movie theater, the territory's correctional
facility, a municipal swimming pool and, of course, a hockey arena.

During our three days there, we met with virtually all the major
territorial and municipal policy-makers, as well as representatives of
an Inuit advocacy group. The two topics that were most important to
everyone were global warming and the Marine Mammal Protection
Act that had been passed by Congress. The law prohibits the impor-
tation into the United States of marine mammal products,
specifically sealskins. The Inuit leaders spoke eloquently of the stark
differences between their subsistence hunting traditions and the
internationally controversial commercial seal hunting practiced in
the North Atlantic off Newfoundland and Labrador. It takes such a

meeting and an on-the-spot visit to appreciate the human and social impact of policies that are formulated far away and that are based on information that is sometimes no better than secondhand.

During the daylight hours the weather was sunny and surprisingly warm. However, when we tried to travel further north to Cumberland Sound and the town of Pangnirtung, our plane had to turn around and return to Iqaluit. Pangnirtung was engulfed in a blinding snowstorm, and there was no way to land safely on the airport's short runway. This was disappointing, but there was some small consolation waiting for us back in Iqaluit, where our errant luggage had arrived. We donned clean clothes and toured a local high school and the Nunavut Arctic College. Jan, of course, made a trip to the Iqaluit Public Library and the Library of the Legislative Assembly. The enthusiasm of the students that we met that day was infectious. If those marvelous young people stay in the territory, then its future will be bright.

Canada is a land of vast resources. Jan and I had occasion to see firsthand the enormous natural wealth of the country on our extensive travels across the provinces and territories. We visited mines, dams, and power-generating facilities in many parts of the country. The ingenuity and technology that we saw was truly awesome.

One of my visits was to Fort McMurray and the Athabaska Tar Sands with our Calgary consul-general, Roy Chavera. We were the guests of Suncor, which has a major interest in the tar sands. In 2002, the US Department of Energy calculated that Canada's proven oil reserves, most of which are in the tar sands, are about 180 billion barrels. That's second only to Saudi Arabia's oil reserves. So when we talk about security of the North American energy supply and weaning our economies from dependence on offshore oil, the tar sands are an important part of the picture.

Recovering this oil has always been a challenge. We visited the tar sands where the earth cover that is over the oil-rich deposits is stripped away. The tar sands are heated to an extremely high temperature and sweet crude oil is separated from the gritty sand. It is an expensive and technology-intensive process, but with world oil prices as high as they've been over the last few years, these oil reserves have become increasingly competitive and important. But as the technology to separate the oil in situ improves, as it will, the recovery rate will also improve and this resource will become an even more important bulwark of our energy security.

Texans say that everything is bigger in their state. They should see the tar sands, where everything is almost unimaginably huge. The reserves cover thousands of square miles. The equipment is the largest in the world. The tires of the dump trucks used to haul the oil-rich sand are several times the height of an average person and each of these trucks can transport about 400 tons at a time. The mechanized shovels use to scrape off the earth cover and dig out the tar sand are the biggest in the world. They may do things in a big way in Texas, but Albertans have a fair claim to be right up there with the best and biggest.

Big is also the word for the uranium mine at McArthur River in northern Saskatchewan. It is the largest in the world, accounting for about 20 percent of the world's uranium production. Jan and I flew to the remote site. We all donned helmets mounted with lamps, overalls and radiation detectors, then took the elevator deep into the earth. The mine is an underground city of roads where virtually all the equipment is operated by remote control. The technological sophistication is world class.

A few months after our visit to Saskatchewan's uranium deposits, I traveled to Sudbury with our new consul-general, Jessica LaCroy, who had arrived in Toronto from a one-year tour of duty in Baghdad, to visit the world famous nickel mines. For decades Sudbury was the world's largest producer of nickel, accounting for close to three-quarters of global production. Other countries have become important producers, but Canada and the Sudbury mines continue to be major world producers.

Sudbury is no longer, of course, just a natural resource community. Its impressive Science North draws visitors from hundreds of miles, and it is also the location of the Sudbury Neutrino Observatory. The observatory records data that has provided revolutionary insights into the properties of neutrinos and the core of the sun. It is highly sophisticated, pure science that relies on a detector built 6,800 feet underground in Inco's Creighton mine outside of Sudbury. You could hardly get a more stark contrast than between this impressive center for research in pure science and the noise and brute scale of the mines. Before you enter the observatory you have to take off all your clothes, shower, and then put on special sterilized clothing. The concern about cleanliness is to reduce background signals from radioactive elements in the mine or that might be brought in from the outside. Such elements could interfere with the weak signal from neutrinos. Cutting edge science in the heart of the Canadian Shield.

Energy has long connected our two economies, and I visited some of the most important sources of energy exported from Canada to the United States. When I was governor of Massachusetts, I flew in a large helicopter to Goldboro where the gas comes ashore from Sable Island off the Nova Scotia coast. This gas became extremely important to the people and industries of my state, helping us stabilize our fuel situation after a winter when we came critically close to running out of energy. After touring the gas processing plant in Goldboro I said to my host, "I've read about Sable Island in *The Perfect Storm*. Why don't we take the helicopter to the island and see the seals and the wild horses and the gas rig?"

"Governor," he answered, "for us to do that you'd have to undergo survival training."

"Survival training? I'm the Republican governor of Massachusetts. Do you really think I need more survival training?"

A few years later, as ambassador to Canada, I finally got a chance to visit Sable Island. It was an hour and a half helicopter trip over tempestuous waves and hazardous ocean currents, with Nova Scotia Lieutenant Governor Myra Freeman, our Halifax consul-general, Steve Kashkett, Jan and I strapped in wearing bright orange search and rescue flight suits and equipped with survival gear and life jackets. Our host, Texas-based ExxonMobil, sent a team of professional search and rescue personnel with us in case we had to land in the dangerous Atlantic waters off Sable Island. Jan was disappointed that we didn't get to test out the suits, which are supposed to provide protection in frigid waters for up to six hours. I didn't share her sense of disappointment.

I would have been disappointed, though, not to see the wildlife for which Sable Island is so famous. Before going out to the Thebaud gas processing platform we landed on the island. There were thousands of seals and the free-roaming Sable Island horses were so close that we could practically touch them. Although it is often claimed that these horses are the descendants of horses that survived some of the hundreds of shipwrecks that took place off the island's shores, historians offer a somewhat less colorful explanation. It seems that they were deliberately introduced to the island by a Boston merchant in the middle of the eighteenth century, along with cattle, hogs and sheep, as part of an unsuccessful effort to establish a farming settlement. Today the horse population of a few hundred is protected by the Canadian government, a contemporary reminder of an interesting chapter from Canada's past.

Even before gas from Sable Island started to flow to my state, Massachusetts was a major consumer of electricity from Quebec. I looked forward to seeing that source of power in the northern reaches of the province near James Bay. When I heard that that we were going to the Radisson I was surprised, but at the same time pleased, that there would be such comfortable accommodations so far north. It turned out that we were going to Radisson, the town, not *the* Radisson.

Radisson sits at the western end of an enormous reservoir created by damming the Grande Rivière and diversions from the Opinaca, Eastmain and Caniapiscau rivers. It is home to the world's largest underground powerhouse and generates electricity from eight water-powered turbine facilities. It is power that is renewable, safe, and clean. Along with our consuls-general from Quebec City and Montreal, Susan Keough and Deborah McCarthy, we flew by helicopter down La Grande Rivière and saw the direct power line that runs all the way to Boston. The next time I'm at a night game at Fenway Park and the lights come on I will think of Radisson and Hydro-Quebec's marvel of engineering. It is a project in which Quebeckers and Canadians take tremendous pride, and rightly so.

Cape Bretoners know that they live in one of the most blessed corners of Canada. The Cabot Trail is a succession of picture postcard views, and there is a joie de vivre among the people of Cape Breton that I found irresistible and welcoming.

Jan and I arrived in time for the Celtic Colours International Festival. Against my better judgment I soon allowed myself to be persuaded onto the dance floor, having a go at step dancing. Jan says that when the music stopped, my partner hobbled off the dance floor and rolled her eyes skyward. Those who have jobs in the River Dance company can rest easy. I won't be joining them any time soon.

Celtic Colours is a Cape Breton Island–wide festival featuring an array of performances that range from square dances in intimate community halls to grand concerts in the island's larger venues. Hundreds of artists from all over the Celtic world, including Wales, Scotland, Ireland, the United States, Brittany and Canada, perform concerts at dozens of venues around the island. Besides the nightly performances there is always a full schedule of workshops on Celtic culture, from playing authentic instruments to sculpture.

We stayed in Cape Breton for the weekend, attending concerts each night and touring the island by day. On the Acadian site of Isle Madame, we visited the historic Notre Dame de l'Assomption church, the Duke of York Cranberry Meadow, the Green Island Distributors fish packing facility, and Samson enterprises, fiberglass boat builders. The vibrancy and the entrepreneurial spirit of the local community were a joy to experience first-hand. It felt just like an election campaign swing, visiting citizens where they work. Jan and I are always comfortable in these settings. It's invigorating to meet people performing the daily tasks that enable them to support their families and contribute to the welfare of their communities. However, the day made me pine a bit for politics and campaigning. I could see that Jan was worried.

On our last day on the island we toured the Highland Village of Iona, where I had made my step dance debut. There we enjoyed a glorious boat cruise on the Bras d'Or Lakes with marine biologist Tim Lambert, members of Parliament Mark Eyking and Roger Cuzner and members of the Bras d'Or Preservation Foundation. The Lakes are salty because of two natural channels and a canal that connect them to the Atlantic Ocean. The unique tidal waters in the Lakes create a rich ecosystem that supports a dazzling array of wildlife.

That evening we attended the Celtic Women concert with Nova Scotia's Lieutenant Governor Myra Freeman and her husband, Larry. The headliner was Cape Breton's own Natalie MacMaster, one of the most recent in a long and illustrious line of performing artists who come from the Island. Jan won the concert's door prize that evening, a Celtic Colours poster signed by the featured performers. Her winning looked somewhat suspicious, but I noticed that she accepted her prize happily and without a murmur of hesitation.

On the long trip back to our hotel in Baddeck late that night, we stopped at a local A&W and ordered my favorite, the Teen Burger. There were six of us in the van, including our Halifax consul-general Len Hill and his wife, Cathy Stevulak, and our RCMP driver and bodyguard. Our drive-through order became a strange exercise in enunciation. I told my driver to order six Teen Burgers, which he did, but it sounded like sixteen burgers. Then it occurred to me: "If they give us 16 burgers instead of six Teen Burgers," I said, "some of us will get only two."

CHAPTER ELEVEN

Still Special, Still Family

My last day as the United States ambassador to Canada, March 18, 2005, was bittersweet for Jan and me. Sad to be leaving one home, happy to be returning to another. Packing to leave the Residence and making arrangements for our return to Massachusetts made us realize once more just how important Canada had become for us. We loved living in Ottawa and we loved traveling through the vast and diverse land that is Canada, representing the president and the people of the United States. Wherever we went we were welcomed. We were in Canada at a particularly critical period, in the wake of the terrorist attacks of September 11, when the world changed and we had a particular role in adapting to that change. So, as much as Jan and I were happy to return home to Hudson, to the family and friends we had always known, we were also sad to leave the people who had become so dear to us and the place that had become our home during the previous four years.

Jan and I joked that we were going from one embassy to another. Our townhouse was still being built when we left Canada, so our home for three months was the Embassy Suites hotel outside of Hudson. We went from a 32-room mansion with chefs to a three-room hotel suite with a kitchenette!

One door closes and another opens. I was stepping down as ambassador, but that did not end my professional connection to Canada. The idea of a job that would enable me to visit Canada often was attractive. When Frank Stronach approached with an offer to join Magna Entertainment Corporation, based in Aurora just north of Toronto, I was interested. I have enormous respect for Frank as a man who, like my grandfather, arrived on this side of the Atlantic with nothing except ambition and a sharp mind for business. Frank has become one of Canada's foremost businessmen, building Magna International into a global auto parts empire that employs over 80,000 people and has annual revenues of over $20 billion.

Frank and I both love racehorses. I suppose that is one of the reasons he thought I'd be the right person for the job as executive vice president of corporate development at Magna Entertainment, which owns some of the most famous racetracks in the United States, including Pimlico Race Course in Maryland, where the Preakness is run; Santa Anita Park in California; and Gulfstream Park in Florida. But I think the more important reason Frank thought I was the right person for the job was because he saw me as a person who could generate constructive debate on a whole range of archaic regulatory aspects of the horse racing industry. I'm pleased that Will Locke, who worked with me at the state house, and the embassy, and is a recent graduate of Tuck School of Business at Dartmouth College, will join me at Magna.

My trademark during my years as ambassador was generating debate. Those who preferred the old style of quiet diplomacy, conducted behind closed doors and out of the public view, didn't always like it. But I know that many Canadians were respectful of my style, and many even seemed to like it. I know this because they told me. As I traveled across the country giving speeches, browsing in airport bookstores waiting for a plane, and when I went out to see a movie in Ottawa or attend a hockey game, people would often come up to me and say, "I agree with you," or "You were right to say what you did." They understood that my straight talk was never disrespectful or unfriendly.

Public diplomacy is not about hectoring or lecturing or criticizing. Even when I was most outspoken, as in my Toronto speech on the Canadian government's decision not to fully support us in Iraq, my words were never intended to be negative or harsh. I just wanted Canadians to know how my government and the American people felt and why. It was a straightforward talk between friends.

When President Bush appointed Karen Hughes, his longtime media and campaign advisor, to the position of undersecretary of state for public diplomacy in January 2005, I think that was a signal that public diplomacy will become an even more prominent tool in the foreign policy of the United States. Everyone acknowledges that America's good image abroad has been threatened over the last few years. The president believes, and I certainly agree, that we need to do a better job getting our side of the story told and letting people throughout the world know what we stand for and what our intentions are.

It starts at the top. When the president goes to Brussels or to the UN and gives a speech on spreading democracy throughout the world, he is engaging in public diplomacy. Telling people where you stand, what you believe in, and advocating particular policies will often generate controversy and attract criticism. But that is what courageous democratic leaders do, and that's what public diplomacy is about. It happened to be a style that suited my personality and my political beliefs, and I was proud to have the opportunity to explain and advocate my government's policies and values to Canadians.

Taking stock of my four years in Canada, I believe my Mission Canada team and I made impressive progress on a number of fronts. I think I got to know Canada and Canadians well, and I acquired a strong attachment to a country that deserves its reputation as a force for good in the world. As a result of those four years, I left with strong ideas about what Canada should do to maintain and increase its influence in the world. This is my last gesture of public diplomacy.

One of the crucial issues that both countries face is energy. The United States gets more oil from Canada than from any other country in the world. We also get a significant amount of natural gas from Canada, about 30 percent of our total consumption. Canada is our single largest foreign supplier of natural gas, but the demand for this resource is growing, in our economies and throughout the world. Even if we bring the Mackenzie Valley and Alaska Slope gas fields on line, it is clear that we will not be able to keep up with the projected demand for natural gas.

Soon there will be large-scale imports of liquefied natural gas from countries such as Nigeria and elsewhere in the world that will have an impact on the price of natural gas in North America. What has been a continental price for natural gas will soon become the world price, as has long been true for oil. Once again there is a global dimension to what we do together. The future development of Canada's natural gas sector will depend in large measure on growth in the American market. But with other supplies of natural gas coming on-stream from various parts of the world, the price of natural gas won't be a made-in-Canada price. It will be set by the worldwide forces of supply and demand for this resource. Long-term contracts for the export of Canadian natural gas to the United States and pipelines to transport that gas to American markets are in both of our national interests as is the location of liquefied natural gas ports.

Energy integration between the two countries is not new. Electricity flows back and forth between Canada and the United States on the power grid that connects us. New England has been the beneficiary of power generated by Hydro-Quebec for many years. I've been to James Bay where this power is generated, and there is a direct current line that runs from James Bay directly to Boston. And I know how important the secure operation of this system is to both our countries. A few weeks before I resigned my post as ambassador, there were stories in the Canadian press about the vulnerability of Hydro-Quebec power lines to terrorist attacks. I believe these stories, and the security problems they raised, point to the need to be vigilant. There are many potential targets of terrorism on both sides of the border. The terrorists must get no opportunity to strike again.

Canada and the United States also have common environmental interests. Our history of working together to protect the natural environment goes back to the creation of the International Joint Commission in 1908. We continue to work together on a number of trans-boundary environmental issues. In recent years both countries have addressed the important problem of climate change. Although our governments have taken different approaches to the Kyoto Treaty, we continue to work together on the International Partnership for a Hydrogen Economy, in the Carbon Sequestration Leadership Forum and on the Global Earth Observation System, all of which attempt to create a monitoring and decision-making framework for dealing with greenhouse gas emissions.

During my tenure in Canada I visited Iqualuit and other northern communities, and I heard directly from the leaders there about the impact that global warming is already having in the Arctic on wildlife habitat. With problem signs already evident in the Arctic, it is clear that if the trend continues there will be problems around the globe. My government believes that we need to get the science right, so we spend close to $6 billion every year on research and monitoring. That's more than is spent by any other country in the world. It is more than is spent by all of Europe, Japan and Canada combined. The United States takes this issue very seriously, and we believe that economic growth is the best way to provide the resources for the environmental investment that will be needed to deal with the consequences of global warming.

Since the attacks of September 11, the United States and Canada have worked closely together to defeat international terrorism. We now have extraordinary cooperation between our law enforcement and intelligence agencies. This is more important than ever. There is some difference between the two countries in public attitudes. In the United States, Americans think that another terrorist strike is probably inevitable. I don't think Canadians are nearly as likely to perceive the terrorist threat as being imminent. But the frontline law enforcement professionals in Canada know that the threat is real. They know that terrorists could use Canada to stage an attack on the United States. And they understand just how devastating the consequences of that would be, for Canada and for us. So it is critically important that Canadian law enforcement agencies continue to have the political support and the resources that they need to do their job, guarding against the terrorist threat before it materializes.

Since the terrorist attacks on New York and Washington, we have seen the steady expansion of the zone of confidence between the two countries. We are working together on exchanging information about who is on the terrorist watch list and who is coming into our countries from abroad. We are working together overseas. Canada and the United States will continue to be welcoming countries—that is part of who we are, part of our histories—but our security standards will now let us discover whom we are welcoming. Hopefully we can prevent the arrival of those who seek to do us harm.

The United States has accepted the Canadian government's decision not to participate in missile defense, but we remain perplexed that Canada would want to give up a decision-making role when matters affecting its sovereignty are potentially at stake. That said, we recognize that is a decision that Canada, and only Canada, can make.

In the meantime, the United States will deploy the system and the United States will protect North America. Critics say that the few tests of the system have not gone well and that it will never work. But that's what they told the Wright brothers, and I've noticed there's been quite a bit of progress in reliable air travel. I'm confident that we will perfect the technology of missile defense as well, and the first steps toward full deployment of the system have already been taken.

More positive, I believe, is the trend toward an increase in Canadian defense spending. The 2005 federal budget was a significant step forward, as are some of the military procurement programs launched in recent years. However, there is still more to do if Canada wants to restore its military stature in the world. One of the first steps involves establishing strategic lift for military deployments abroad. Today Canada is a consumer of strategic lift; when the Canadian Forces need to move troops and equipment to crisis spots around the world, they must rent the airplanes or travel with another country's forces. When the tsunami disaster struck Asia and Canada wanted to send its DART team to help, it was Russian transport planes that carried them there. The delay in getting Canadian aid to the disaster zone was because the Canadian military had to first find transport. Not only should a country like Canada not have to count on other countries to transport soldiers and equipment, it should be able to help smaller countries get their forces to trouble spots and crisis zones when the need arises. This ought to be a priority for Canada.

Another area where Canadian military efforts should be focused is in the high technology field of command and control computers, communications, intelligence, surveillance and reconnaissance, what the military calls C4ISR. Canada develops many leading edge technologies, both military and industrial. When a response is needed to an international crisis, many countries can deploy troops, but far fewer have the latest satellite communications, intelligence systems, computers and other necessary surveillance systems. This enabling technology is every bit as important as the infantry and peacekeepers needed for trouble spots, and is also less manpower intensive.

A third way in which the Canadian military could excel would be through its special operations forces. Canada's elite, Tier 1 JTF2, is as capable as any Tier 1 Special Force in the world. It makes a significant contribution wherever it is deployed. I think Canada should invest in a Tier 2 special operations capability. A Tier 2 Special Operations unit—small, lean, quickly deployable, and highly trained, with the latest communications and technologies—would make sense for Canada. Such a unit could be deployed in numbers that would allow sustainable deployments of highly capable fighters. Such a unit could also perform softer missions, such as aiding civil authorities. These Tier 2 Special Operations forces are in constant demand in NATO and for peacekeeping operations worldwide.

Energy, environmental protection, security at home and the ability to protect our interests abroad are important areas of cooperation between Canada and the United States. But there is also our shared goal of building a better world through the spread of freedom and prosperity. I strongly believe that the globalization of free trade is the path toward creating stable democracies and improved economic well-being for more of the world's peoples. The first step is to help countries create an encouraging climate for investment and trade; that in turn will generate jobs and prosperity and a better life for their people. It is a step that Canada and the United States took through NAFTA, forging a partnership with Mexico that has produced billions of dollars in new investment, millions of jobs and a growing middle class in that country. Canada and the United States are countries with high standards of living. We should never lose sight of the fact that most of the world's people do not enjoy anything close to our level of affluence. I believe that helping other countries improve their economies, lifting people out of poverty, is the right thing to do. Not only is it the right thing to do morally, it is in our economic interest to do so. Canada and the United States are successful exporting countries. If we continue to invest in education, training and technology we will create increased productivity and we will create more and better-paying jobs than we will ever lose through outsourcing.

Helping the poorer countries of the world improve their economic situation is also in our security interests. For example, in Afghanistan we are trying to create a climate for investment and trade — a climate that includes democracy and the rule of law. We want people there to have a voice in their own future and an opportunity to improve their own lives and the lives of their children; at the same time companies will have confidence in making investments there. If we are successful in that endeavor, it is much less likely that Afghanistan will ever again become a training ground for terrorists. Where there is prosperity and hope, terrorist organizations will not be able to recruit new members for their cause.

We should always remember when we talk about free trade, economic globalization and the expansion of open markets, that trade and investment figures dwarf foreign aid figures. We can use foreign aid to help a country create a judicial system that respects the rule of law. We can use foreign aid to help a country build a road to provide access to a resource that will help its economy grow. But we will not lift people out of poverty through foreign aid. We need trade and investment to do that. Only with trade and investment will countries develop economies that produce the jobs and prosperity that lift people out of poverty.

In his second inaugural address, President Bush spoke about fundamental values and their place in the world. The winds of freedom are blowing throughout the world, he said, bringing down the repressive regimes that deny their people the dignity and opportunity that only democracy can ensure. He noted that the value of freedom is not uniquely American. There are, the president said, many paths to democracy and no single best form of democratic government. But the hope for democracy, he said, is universal. The belief in human dignity, in the worth of every individual as an individual, and in the right to self-government, are universal values. They can only be sustained by the constant application of the rule of law, including the protection of minorities and the right of all people to free dissent.

History is showing that the president is right and that the policies of his administration are helping people in countries throughout the world reach for and achieve those aspirations. We have seen Palestinians elect a new leader, President Mahmoud Abbas, in a free election. We have witnessed the will of the people prevail in the Ukraine. In Afghanistan, a country where a little more than three years ago women had no role in the society, no one had the right to vote, and one of the most repressive regimes of modern times ruled, men and women lined up by the thousands and voted by the millions because they want to be free. And then in Iraq, despite the great dangers that voters in many parts of the country faced, Iraqis turned out in astounding numbers to register their support for democracy.

We know that the path to freedom is not always easy. The challenges have been enormous in Afghanistan and Iraq, and the price has been paid in lives, including the lives of Canadian and American soldiers. This is a very heavy price to pay. The burden is great, but the goal is worthy, it is noble, and it is attainable. Canada and the United States have an obligation to help bring freedom around the world. Our nations can help those countries with unstable governments and failing economies to make the transition to democracy and open markets, and in doing so set them on the path toward stability and prosperity and a better life for their people. This, I believe, is the challenge for Canada, a country with a proud tradition of internationalism. It is not a tradition that is upheld by a weakened military. It is a tradition that has always depended on a strong military and the willingness to back up words with the force of arms.

Freedom is not free: it carries a price. That price is the willingness and the capacity to oppose freedom's enemies at home and abroad and to support the natural and legitimate aspirations of peoples throughout the world to live lives of dignity. These peoples sometimes need our help, and we must be ready to come to their aid. As President Bush said, "It is the calling of our time." And it is an endeavor in which Canada should continue to play a major role.

———————

A week after I stepped down as ambassador, Prime Minister Martin made his first visit to President Bush's ranch in Crawford, Texas. He and Mexican President Vicente Fox had been invited to discuss trade and security issues and the future direction of the NAFTA partnership. Like everyone else, I read in the papers about what took place at Crawford. For the first time in four years I was on the outside looking in.

I was heartened, though, by the clear evidence of progress that had been made on several of the issues that I had worked on from that day in the spring of 2001 when I had presented my credentials to Governor General Adrienne Clarkson at the Citadel in Quebec City. The prime minister expressed enthusiasm about further development of Alberta's enormous tar sands oil reserves for export to the United States, calling this a "great, great opportunity." The three leaders issued a joint statement that essentially built on the Smart Border Action Plan that I had helped draft in the months after the September 11 terrorist attacks. The tone of the meeting was positive in a way that did not try to paper over the differences that we continued to have on some issues. From the several meetings that I had with the president during my time as United States ambassador to Canada, I know that he understood well the positions and concerns that Prime Minister Martin would have expressed at Crawford. I thought the prime minister put it well when he said that the amazing thing is that our governments don't have *more* and *sharper* disagreements, given the sheer volume of all that our countries do together.

Even the optics of the meeting were good. President Bush presented the prime minister with a pair of leather cowboy boots, embroidered with the Canadian, American and Mexican flags. Prime Minister Martin invited the president to visit his farm in Quebec's eastern townships. The special relationship once again seemed to be special. The truth is that it had never stopped being special.

Along with a wealth of memories, many new friends, a small mountain of books and a Canadian son-in-law, Jan and I brought back to Massachusetts another souvenir of the country that we came to think of as home. It was a diamond that I bought for Jan when we visited the Ekati diamond mine in the Northwest Territories. Chad Yesue, my godson and a remarkable young jeweler, mounted it on a gold ring that Jan wears on her wedding finger. It is what's called a "conflict-free" diamond. A microscopic polar bear design is laser-etched into the girdle of the diamond to show that the diamond does not come from a country where the illegal trade in diamonds is used to fund rebel groups. It's a type of diamond found in Canada and symbolizes for us much of what the country stands for: a wealth of natural resources, striking beauty and ideals of peace. This treasured piece of Canada serves as a daily reminder of the wonderful years we spent among people who made us feel like family.

Before I left Ottawa I received a letter from Condoleezza Rice, the US secretary of state. It was a warm farewell letter with an important message about Canada:

> Our relationship with Canada is the most complex we have with any country, given our extensive border, bilateral trade and bi-national defense issues. Your tenure has been exceptionally challenging, beginning as it did shortly before 9/11. In the days after those terrorist attacks, yours was the defining image of America for most Canadians: the same combination of profound grief and firm determination that the president demonstrated.

Then and in the years since, your consistent and firm-but-neighborly efforts with the Canadian government and people have advanced American interests in improving our shared security and enhancing our outstanding commercial relations. I know from the Canadian press that even those who are disinclined to agree with the policies of the United States have admired your willingness to tackle difficult issues and to speak openly and frankly about them.

What particularly pleased me about Condi's letter was the final sentence in which she saluted "your willingness to tackle difficult issues and to speak openly and frankly about them." The secretary of state is the president's most important advocate for public diplomacy. She believed that I had fulfilled my mission to represent well my president and my country to our nation's closest friend, Canada.

Index